THE DEATH OF THE BRAHMIN LIBERAL

A biographical montage of the Rt. Hon'ble V.S. Srinivasa Sastri (1869-1946)

M. K.SUDARSHAN

BlueRose ONE.com
Stories Matter
NewDelhi • London

BLUEROSE PUBLISHERS
India | U.K.

For permissions requests or inquiries regarding this publication,
please contact:

BLUEROSE PUBLISHERS
www.BlueRoseONE.com
info@bluerosepublishers.com
+91 8882 898 898
+4407342408967

ISBN: 978-93-7310-043-2

Cover Design: Aman Sharma
Typesetting: Manisha Rawat

First Edition: October 2025

Contents

Disclaimer

The Rt. Hon'ble V.S. Srinivasa Sastri (*1869-1946*)

1 M.K Sudarshan

Author's Preface

At the outset, let me make it clear that this book is not intended to be a new biography of the Rt. Hon'ble V.S. Srinivasa Sastri.

No new research material has been unearthed from the historical archives about Sastri's life and work; nor should this book be regarded as any fresh or original assessment of the man or of the yeoman service he rendered to India in his lifetime. This book is exactly what its title claims to be: a ***montage*** of my own glimpses into the life of Srinivasa Sastri —no more, no less.

There are excellent biographical sources in the public domain, both digital and textual, that are easily available and on which I have relied while writing this biographical montage which is, in a more real and substantial sense, my own tribute to Srinivasa Sastri. The sources are listed below:

a. **Letters Of the Right Honourable V. S. Srinivasa Sastri (1944)** by ***Jagadisan T. N.***; Publication date 1944: Geography Biography History, C-DAC, Noida; Publisher Asia Publishing House, Bombay: digitallibraryindia; JaiGyan

b. **The Right Honourable V.S. Srinivasa Sastri – A Political Biography** by K. Kodanda Rao: Asia Publishing House

c. Digital archives of the **Gokhale Institute of Politics and Economics** (https://gipe.ac.in/

d. **Kamala Devi Lectures**: by Srinivasa Sastri (1935) - University of Calcutta

e. **G.V. Gundappa on Srinivasa Sastri**: https://www.prekshaa.in/VS-Srinivasa-Sastri-Part- published as a series by Preksha (a Journal of Culture and Philosophy)

f. Personal anecdotes shared with me by **Sri. G. Karthikeyan**, Chartered Accountant, and the son of Srinivasa Sastri's maternal grand-daughter *Smt. Padmini Gopalan.* 'Her cousin Smt.

Rajeshwari' *Vijayan* was kind enough to pen a *Foreword* on behalf of Sastri's family. *Karthik*, as I call him today, has remained my very good friend for the last forty odd years. Another distant relative of Sastri's family, and another good friend of mine, **Sri. Harish Devarajan** (*Leadership Coach* M/s People Unlimited) has also penned a very affectionate tribute to Sastri.

g. In fleshing out a few of my narratives and commentaries in this book, I also took occasional assistance from online AI research tools.

**** ****

Srinivasa Sastri himself was too a shy and private person to want anyone to write his biography. He was said to have requested his admiring friend, the renowned Kannada scholar, playwright and historian, G.V. Gundappa (GVG), more than once that no biography of his should be written by anybody.

Sastri set very high standards for how a biography of any person ought to be written and summed up his view by insisting that a biography should portray its hero as he was and not as the biographer would have wished him to be. While bringing out his good points, his defects should not be overlooked.

"Our heroes and heroines," said Sastri, *"can well stand just as they are at the judgment-bar of history. Their good has gone to their achievement and their evil as well.... The contribution of the sound and the unsound makes up contemporary life...Let our sense of human values be robust. Let us be to our children in the pages of biography and autobiography no better and no worse than they see us in everyday life".*

Later in his life, Sastri however broke his own rule and began penning his autobiography in a series of articles for a popular Tamil magazine, "***Swadesamitran***". The series was then published as a book with the title: ***"Meendum vaazhndhaal***".... *"If I were to live again"*. And he justified breaking the rule in untypically gushing, overly self-defensive and self-exculpatory words:

"The autobiography is not so obviously out of court. Time was when I would have run away from the idea as an outrageously immodest proposal. I realise the

plea of virginity is no longer available. Alas, I have fallen. And to whom? You don't expect an old man to grow poetic over his senile amours. Yet, believe me, this Tamil escapade warms my blood with genuine passion. It is awkward, stumbling and --don't I see? — ludicrous. But it possesses me for the time. I am oblivious of what the critical world says. What does it matter so long as I am thrilled? If second childhood may lisp, let it lisp in the mother-tongue. But I must not wander.

"Aren't they (the critical world) a wee bit human in heaven? What a question! It is rank blasphemy. But I mean, when they sternly interrogate me on my vanity at seventy-two, to plead that my lapse is a mere peccadillo and cite precedents from the annals of Vishnu and Indra! I hope they have still the decency to blush.

"An autobiography in English would be utterly naked and defenceless. I have not forgotten 'the ocean of mercy' and all that sort of thing. Would it avail one who has registered an oath in Chitragupta's book and endorsed it solemnly?"

**** ****

Sastri's breaking his own rule on writing biographies and autobiographies – calling his own *"lapse" "a mere peccadillo"* – thus emboldened me to re-read, revisit accounts of his life-history that were so readily made available to me by my friend and Sastri's great-grandson, Karthik, and which were in the public digital-space as well, and then begin to write this montage of biographical impressions of the man and his work.

It was not my main purpose in this book to recount Sastri's life in its entirety. The focus instead was solely on Sastri's deeply held and openly professed **Classical Liberal** values of the 19th-20th century CE to which many contemporaneous political leaders and the cultural intelligentsia of India also swore allegiance. It was very fascinating for me discover how seamlessly and graciously Sastri was able to wear his strikingly **Brahminical**-background beliefs along with the best of modern Liberal ideas and ideals but without ever seeming to wear either of them on his sleeves. In hindsight and from the perspective of identity-politics, Sastri's character and personality seemed to defy the popular narrative we hear today so much about that *"if you are a Brahmin, you cannot be a Liberal… and vice versa"*.

Throughout this biographical montage, the reader will thus be able to appreciate why I have expressed admiration for this unique ***Brahmin-Liberal*** of the last century in India's Pre-Independence history.

Today in the 21st century, both *Brahmin- and Classical-Liberalism* have become virtually extinct. Men of Sastri's mould in the rough-and-tumble of the competitive, *no-holds-barred* and *do-anything-to-win* world of Indian politics are rarities indeed. So, the narratives that I have myself woven into this book, might possibly come across to the reader as though they are far too facile answers conjured up for the central question I pose myself:

"If Srinivasa Sastri were reborn to live today in India --- "meendum vaazhndhaal", to use his own curious Tamil expression --- how might he have been able to square his catholic Brahmin-Liberal "weltanschauung" with the Indian zeitgeist as I know it today?"

The final chapter of this book, I hope will speak for itself while giving the reader, as he turns its very past page, enough and more food for thought to come to his or her own conclusion about such an imponderable question.

****

Now to end my preface, just a few words on the title given to this book.

A few very good friends of mine expressed their uneasiness with my using the word "***Death***" in the book's title. "*It sounds morbid*", they felt. They suggested alternatives such as: "*Decline*"; or "*The Last of the Brahmin Liberal*" (like the "*Last of the Mohicans*"!). One dear friend asked me also to drop the word "*brahmin*" and replace it with the more anodyne synonym, "*intellectual*".

I was acutely sensitive to what my friends were mutedly but implicitly trying to tell me. *"Death of Brahmin-Liberal"* could be easily misconstrued by readers as death of the very memory of Srinivasa Sastri; and that would be not only unkind to him but also inaccurate. It was also a very inauspicious expression to use while referring to him. However, after dwelling seriously upon the friendly suggestions given, I decided to persist in the title already chosen. I, however, did owe them all an explanation, which I did.

The word "*death*" in a book's title can and does make a reader perhaps squirm and shift uncomfortably in the chair. I am very aware the unnerving effect my book's title might have on readers' minds. However, I choose to persist with the title chosen because I am convinced it serves the central purpose of the book *viz.:* to describe the death of decency and decorum, idealism and Dharmic values in politics and public life today in our country. When a tiger has already gone extinct as a species in our beautiful wildlife forestlands, what does it matter whether we call the extinction "*Death*" or "*The Last of the Tiger*"?

"*Death*" is the title, incidentally, of several notable works in literary, historical and philosophical works across the world. Most famously, here are a few examples: (a) "*Dialogue with Death*": the Katha Upanishad; (b) by *Arthur Koestler* (c) *Eknath Eswaran* (d) "*Death in Venice*" by *Thomas Mann* (d) "*Death be not proud*" and "*Death's Duel*" – both by *John Donne*....

This book is thus not about the demise of Srinivasa Sastry's memory... It is about the death of Sastri's balanced *Brahmin-Liberal model of Indian Polity.* This book is not to mourn the death of Sastri. It is to commemorate his *Dharmic Idealism*...

M.K. Sudarshan

Chennai: *September 1, 2025.*

Foreword & Tributes

A Loving Tribute to Sri. V.S. Srinivasa Sastri (VSS) by surviving members of his family today: (collective reminiscences of Smt. Rajeshwari Raji Vijayan (great granddaughter, Smt. Padmini Gopalan (granddaughter) and Sri. G. Karthikeyan (great grandson)

I feel honoured and humbled to write this note on V.S. Srinivasa Sastri, who was the father of my maternal grandmother, Rukmini. My mother Alamelu was Rukmini's eldest child, and she spent a lot of time with her grandparents. She loved and revered both and became imbued with their values too.

As her children, all four of we sisters heard a lot about *"thaatha's"* values of austerity, simplicity and scholarship. We also read a lot about Lakshmi (Mrs Sastri), her patience, her cheerfulness and her total control of temper. Nobody has ever seen her get angry or shout. They were thus both always held up as examples for us to follow in life.

What are the values he, VSS, lived by? While reading **Bhagavad Gita** *Chapter 17*, the *Shloka* numbering 14, 15 and 16 struck me as exactly describing those values, adhering to which is called "*Tapas*" in Sanskrit, translated as *Austerity* in English.

देवद्विजगुरुप्राज्ञपूजनं शौचमार्जवम् |
ब्रह्मचर्यमहिंसा च शारीरं तप उच्यते || 14||

deva-dwija-guru-prājña- pūjanaṁ śhaucham ārjavam
brahmacharyam ahinsā cha śhārīraṁ tapa uchyate

(Gist): Worship of the Gods, of the twice born, of teachers, and of the wise; purity, uprightness, continence and non-injury; these are said to be the austerities of the body.

अनुद्वेगकरं वाक्यं सत्यं प्रियहितं च यत् |
स्वाध्यायाभ्यसनं चैव वाङ्मयं तप उच्यते || 15||

anudvega-karaṁ vākyaṁ satyaṁ priya-hitaṁ cha yat
svādhyāyābhyasanaṁ chaiva vāṅ-mayaṁ tapa uchyate

(Gist): The speech that causes no excitement, which is truthful, pleasant, and beneficial, and also the study of sacred books, recitation - these form austerity of speech.

मनः प्रसादः सौम्यत्वं मौनमात्मविनिग्रहः |
भावसंशुद्धिरित्येतत्तपो मानसमुच्यते || 16||

manaḥ-prasādaḥ saumyatvaṁ maunam ātma-vinigrahaḥ
bhāva-sanśhuddhir ity etat tapo mānasam uchyate

(Gist): Serenity of mind, gentleness, silence, self-control, and purity of disposition – all these are mental tapas.

All these qualities describe the *Sattvic* personality. And all these qualities were present in V.S.S. in abundant measure.

****

Sastri's life was not easy. As the eldest son he had to support his mother, his widowed elder sister with her children as well as two younger brothers. He shouldered the responsibilities without complaint.

At the age of twenty-one, his wife Parvathi died in childbirth leaving him with a baby boy (V.S. Sankaran). He then re-married Lakshmi who brought up the baby lovingly. Lakshmi had two daughters, Rukmini and Savithri. Savitri however died at the age of twelve. Only Rukmini survived.

Rukmini (my grandmother) was married to Sundaram, the son of his dear friend Seshu. *No dowry, no horoscope matching*! Rukmini and Sundaram had four daughters and three sons.

During all these years V.S.S was fired by the great desire to serve his country. He joined the **Servants of India Society** and sincerely worked for it for the rest of his life.

It involved great sacrifice for his wife who never dreamed of complaining. He then went on to occupy so many high posts with magnificent salaries, which were all given away to the *Servants of India Society*. Luckily for the family, both Sastri's son and son-in-law were employed in good jobs, and the family was thus always well-to-do and comfortable. V.S. Sankaran was in the Postal Department, retiring as *Post-Master General of the Madras Presidency*. Son-in-law Sundaram served and retired as *Agent, the Imperial Bank of India*.

(Sitting: *Rukmani Sundaram (daughter of Sastri); standing left to right, daughters Kalpakam Raman, Padmini Gopalan, Lakshmi Narayanaswami and Alamelu Padmanabhan).*

Vineet Thakur in his book "*The first Indian Diplomat*" has described "*thaatha's*" extensive travels worldwide on work and the burdens and troubles he undertook for the sake of the welfare of the Indian Diaspora throughout much of his career as a diplomat. It was mostly from the years 1919 through 1922 and it involved travelling by steamer-ship to Japan, Canada, U.S.A, and of course, to England several times. The journeys must have been long and tedious, but Sastri never complained. As **Agent General of India in S. Africa**, his work became well known. While working there in that country, Sastri was successful in raising much needed public funds and used it to establish an educational college for the Indian children living there. This College **in Durban, The Sastri College**, in fact, will be proudly celebrating its **Centenary Year in 2029.**

In politics, Sastri was cautious and pragmatic in his approach. He believed solely in Constitutional methods. He didn't approve of *dharna* and such other methods. He warned Gandhiji that it will all go against us (the country) in the future. Despite their differences, Gandhiji, however, always loved and respected VSS, and fondly called him his *"elder brother"*. Interestingly, V.S.S was born on **22 Sept 1869** and Gandhiji on **Oct 2, 1869**.

Sastri was basically a scholar and an intellectual. He admired the English language and literature but never got Westernized. He loved the *Tamil Sangam* and Tamil literature too. The *Webster's Dictionary* and *Valmiki Ramayana* were always beside him on his table.

It is here that I wish to take the opportunity to mention my aunt, *Smt. Padmini Gopalan*, my mother's younger sister, who also like *"thaatha"* himself, was fired by the great desire to work for the underprivileged people of our society. She remains even today a spark of the old flame! For Smt. Padmini, Montessori way of learning was more than teaching—it was hope. Her unwavering spirit helped children discover the joy of learning, no matter their circumstances. Very few people today seem to appreciate the fact that instilling good values at a young age ensures the development of valuable adults later in society. It is difficult to develop good values, truthfulness, sincerity, honesty etc. unless it is shown by example to young children at a very young age.

VSS was a true Hindu, but he had no time for very orthodox superstitions. He was against child marriage and helped in passing the landmark **Sarada Act**. He was firmly against the Indian Dowry system and was deeply saddened by young girls being ill-treated by in-laws within conservative families on that account. Some of the earliest encounters of his with the ills of society are stories are precisely about this system.

Another encounter of his against the orthodoxy was this: In those days it was considered a sin for a Brahmin to cross the seas and travel abroad. On his return, Sastri was forced thus by the orthodoxy to perform certain rites of repentance and penance which he refused.

An interesting anecdote in this regard was repeated to me by my aunt, *Padmini Gopalan.* It used to be the dream of every Hindu --- and perhaps it remains that even today — to visit the holy city of Kasi on a pilgrimage at least once in a lifetime. A few of Lakshmi *patti's* relatives were going thus to Kasi. They invited her to go along with them. She happily agreed. They commented that it will give her a chance to do *prayaschittam* (ritual atonement) for all the sins of her husband (who had committed the sin of many times crossing the seas and going abroad!). When Lakshmi *patti* heard about it, she became very offended and refused to go on the pilgrimage. Her reasoning, she said, was *"my husband did no wrong… He was only doing good work for society and for the country at large"*.

These are just a few my little glimpses into the life of a great man who had been blessed with a good wife too… And both of whom cared so dearly for world welfare more than for their own personal comfort. Today, I feel that my entire family is blessed to be able to claim such noble souls as our ancestors.

Mrs. Rajeshwari Vijayan

September 17, 2025, Chennai, INDIA.

*** *** ***

A Tribute

Throughout my childhood and even in my adulthood days, I have heard from my father R. Devarajan, interesting incidents from the life of his great - granduncle Rt. Hon. VS Srinivasa Sastry. My father used to be proud that he was a scion of the great man.

The very first inter-collegiate contest that I participated in, representing *Vivekananda College*, Chennai, was the **'Srinivasa Sastry memorial Oratorical contest'** conducted by the **'Servants of India Society'** at the Sanskrit College premises in Mylapore. It was a proud moment for my father and his uncles, *S.K. Sivaraman* and *S.K. Rajaraman* (grandnephews of the great man himself) who were also present at the venue, to hear me speak and win the first prize at this event, in memory of an ancestor very close to their hearts.

When Sudarshan, a dear friend and former colleague of mine, first shared his blogs about Srinivasa Sastry and his multi - faceted life, I was reminded of the stories I had heard and read.

In this book, Sudarshan has woven a fine tapestry of history in a very engaging and informative style. He has taken exceptional efforts to share facts and artifacts that bring out the significant role played by the protagonist in different contexts.

The special relationship and mutual respect that existed between Sastry and Mahatma Gandhi is highlighted so well with the select rally of letters between them, during key moments of our nation's history.

Sastry's distinct values, abilities and attitude which define his character, his contributions and the way he faced challenges have been brought out quite well. The unapologetic way in which Sastry led his life, true to his conscience and commitments, is also beautifully showcased.

Sudarshan has presented objectively, both the liberal and orthodox dimensions of Sastry across the realms of politics, international diplomacy, religion, social justice, and Brahminical lifestyle. He builds a strong proposition that this kind of unique blend in one person is rare to find and now almost extinct.

This book provides an insightful exposition of the life and legacy of Rt. Hon. V.S. Srinivasa Sastry, a true statesman!

Harish Devarajan

Leadership Coach (www.peopleunlimited.in)

Chapter 1
The Sastri College, Durban, Centenary Year 2029

The Sastri College in Durban, South Africa is a co-educational, multi-racial, multi-cultural state secondary school with learners from grade 8 to grade 12. The founding of Sastri College was the vision of the (Late) **Rt. Hon'ble V.S Srinivasa Sastri** (1869-1946 CE). The official opening of the school took place on **Monday, 14th October 1929** when the Earl of Athlone, Governor-General of South Africa inaugurated it https://sastricollege.co.za/about-us/. The College represented the vision of Sri. Srinivasa Sastri – who was then the *Agent General of the Government of India* in South Africa – to realise which the Indian Community in South Africa collected and contributed the handsome amount of 18,000 sterling pounds. The school is today located on the periphery of the central business district of the City of Durban. It is a school rich in tradition and respected for its high academic achievement. The website of the Sastri College says this proudly: *"These have been handed down to us through the dedication and vision of our predecessors which continues to inspire us today"*.

On October 10, 2029, the Sastri College, Durban will celebrate its Centenary Year.

My very dear and long-time friend and fellow Chartered Accountant, **Sri. G. Karthikeyan** is the maternal great-grandson of Rt. Hon'ble Srinivasa Sastri. Yesterday, ***Karthik*** (as I have always called him) proudly informed me that the Administration of the Sastri College, Durban, had been so very gracious to send in, a full three years in advance (!), a formal invitation to his mother *Smt. Padmini Gopalan*, Sri. Srinivasa Sastri's granddaughter, to attend the **Centenary Year Celebrations** of the college in October 2029! Karthik's message to me was: *"Sudarshan, as an aside, the Ambassador of South Africa to India Mr. Anil Sooklal contacted my mother to inform her that they are planning the* *centenary celebration of Sastri College in 2029 at Durban. He wanted to invite the Sastri family to Durban for the Centenary celebration..."*

"*How ever so gracious of the Sastri College, Durban!*" I thought! And how grateful they must be to the memory of Srinivasa Sastri that the institution has not forgotten him or his surviving family in India today... even 100 years after it was founded! I replied to Karthik immediately, expressing my fulsome praise for the South African college for their gesture towards his mother and the entire family of Rt. Hon'ble Srinivasa Sastri. I told him I hoped that come October 2029, he will travel to Durban to attend the Centenary festivities of the Sastri College as a mark of respect to the memory of his great-grandfather.

The above exchange of correspondence with Karthik reminded of my own great admiration for Sri. Srinivasa Sastri. Although I am a student of Indian history during the period of India's freedom struggle, I had not acquainted myself too well or too deeply with Srinivasa Sastri's own role in it. Everything I knew about Sastri was from what is out there in the public domain which, of course, anyone can easily access:

Srinivasa Sastri was born to a poor temple priest in the village of Valangaiman near Kumbakonam, India. He completed his education at Kumbakonam and worked as a schoolteacher and later, headmaster (The Hindu High School) in Triplicane, Madras. He entered politics in 1905 when he joined the ***Servants of India Society****. Sastri served as a member of the* ***Indian National Congress*** *from 1908 to 1922 but later resigned in protest against the* ***non-cooperation movement****. Sastri was one of the founding members of the* ***Indian Liberal Party****. In his later days, he was strongly opposed to the partition of India.*

Srinivasa Sastri served as a member of the ***Madras Legislative Council*** *from 1913 to 1916,* ***Imperial Legislative Council of India*** *from 1916 to 1919 and the* ***Council of State*** *from 1920 to 1925. Sastri also functioned as* ***India's delegate to the League of Nations****, as member of the* ***Privy Council of the United Kingdom*** *and* ***Agent to the Union of South Africa.***

**** ****

However, my admiration for Srinivasa Sastri did not stem from whatever little I knew of his work in Indian politics in the Pre-Independence era.

When I was a young man in my early 30s, I had grown to admire him greatly when I had first read a book, a compilation of Srinivasa Sastri's famous **"Lectures on the Ramayana,"** delivered over several months (April through November 1944) at the **Madras Sanskrit College**.

Reading that book (https://a.co/d/1wvVj6u) was my very first introduction to not only the "*itihaasa's*" magnificence as an ancient epic but also to the exquisiteness of **Maharishi Valmiki's** Sanskrit language. More importantly, the lectures of Srinivasa Sastri opened my eyes for the very first time in life to the immense possibilities of the many ways of understanding and creatively appreciating the *Ramayana*'s literary and scriptural profundity with the aid of English cadence of which Sastri was an unequalled master. For someone like me who had no more than a mere smattering knowledge of the Sanskrit language, *Valmiki Ramayana* was brought so vividly alive indeed thanks to the sheer brilliance of Sri. Srinivasa Sastri's *Lectures.*

Many years later, I myself authored and published a book of essays titled *"The Unusual Essays of an Unknown Sri Vaishnava"* (2025 edition: https://amzn.in/d/awRFQuB. The couple of essays on the *Ramayana* that I had penned therein, I must acknowledge, did borrow quite a lot and did quote profusely from Sastri's own "*Lectures*". So great was the spell of inspiration that Rt. Hon'ble Srinivasa Sastri always had cast upon me, indeed, in my own humble literary forays!

**** ****

Upon receiving such wonderful, glad news from my friend Karthik about the upcoming **2029 Sastri College Centenary Celebrations in Durban**, my mind also turned a little sombre when I began to wistfully recall the history of India's freedom struggle and Srinivasa Sastri's own distinguished albeit chequered and, sadly, under-appreciated role in it. It is in that mood that I feel compelled to boldly say too here that I feel, back here in India -- *especially in Tamil Nadu* whose illustrious son of the soil he truly was -- the memory of the Rt. Hon'ble Srinivasa Sastri, for some unfathomable reason, has not received half the reverence and celebration that the *Sastri College* in faraway Durban has deemed fit to accord him during its Centenary year celebrations in 2029.

To fathom and to try to understand the reason might perhaps force me to revisit and dig a little bit, at least, into that chapter in India's Pre-Independence history in which Sastri was made a major player by none other than the *Father of the Nation*, **Mahatma Gandhi.** In fact, the best place from which to start digging a bit into that history, I would say, is to discover an intimate piece of correspondence that took place between Gandhi and Sastri ... a letter in which the Mahatma virtually hustled a reluctant Sastri to undertake a very important and historic political assignment in South Africa.

My friend Karthik yesterday fished out that letter dated **April 1927** and sent it across to me in which the Mahatma had written to his great-grandfather:

6th April 1927

My dear Friend

This is from a sick bed. I had hoped to see you . Bangalore and press my suit. But it cannot be for some time yet. I have no reply to my wire which I hope you did get. You will break the heart of Indians in South Africa if you do not go. Mrs Sastri should certainly go with you.[7] I do not know that it is an advantage to have both host and hostess as brilliant talkers in English. You will be her interpreter or you can take for her one of the gifted Tamil graduate girls of whom you have so many. She will be her companiou, teacher and interpreter. What did Queen Victoria do when she was hostess to the Shah of Persia who knew no English? And you can make it clear to Lord Irwin that you would want to be here when

7 In the event Mrs Sastri did not accompany Mr Sastri.

78 LETTERS OF SRINIVASA SASTRI

the Royal Commission comes. Lastly, there will be no fear of pin-pricks whilst Lord Irwin is Viceroy. He knows you so well. I urge you to re-consider your decision and go even if it is for a year. You alone can inaugurate the working of tbe compact, you alone can set the tone.

May God guide you.

Yours sincerely

M. K. GANDHI

This correspondence, written by **Mahatma Gandhi to V. S. Srinivasa Sastri on 6th April 1927,** centres around Gandhi urging Sastri to reconsider his decision about not going to South Africa to represent Indian interests. Gandhi expresses personal disappointment at not being able to meet Sastri due to illness but strongly emphasizes the importance of Sastri's visit for the morale and well-being of Indians in South Africa.

Gandhi is persuasive, mentioning that Sastri's absence would deeply disappoint the Indian community there. He discusses logistical details, such as the presence of Mrs. Sastri or a suitable interpreter, reflecting the complexities of diplomatic responsibilities abroad. Gandhi draws on historical references (*such as Queen Victoria hosting the Shah of Persia!*) to argue that language barriers could be overcome and should not deter Sastri from making the trip.

Further, Gandhi addresses the broader political context: he refers to the upcoming Royal Commission and the political climate under Lord Irwin, the Viceroy, indicating that Sastri's leadership set the right tone and inaugurate the '*working of the compact*' between India and South Africa. Gandhi earnestly urges Sastri to reconsider his decision, even if only for a year, stating, ***"You alone can inaugurate the working of the compact, you alone can set the tone."*** He concludes with a blessing for divine guidance.

From a careful reading of the above letter of Gandhi, we can easily conclude that Srinivasa Sastri's influence on Gandhi's political strategies was very strong in several nuanced ways, especially during the 1920s when Indian nationalist leaders like Gandhi, Gokhale and Nehru were negotiating the complex terrain of colonial politics and international diplomacy.

**** **** ****

Chapter 2
Ends and Means

Throughout the 1920s and 1930s, the mass leaders of the Indian National Congress who were at the forefront of the Freedom Struggle against British Colonial Rule all fell into three broad but clear ideological groupings. They were all patriots devoted to the cause of Independence, but they differed sometimes quite widely in their respective approach towards how the struggle must be waged. The end was one, but the means were varied.

In that broad spectrum of freedom fighters, at one extreme were arrayed those like **Veer Savarkar, Bhagath Singh and Subhas Chandra Bose,** to name only a few, who made no secret of their choice to take up arms against the British Government in India. At the other end of the spectrum were those aligned with Gandhi's non-violent *satyagraha* approach -- which included ceaseless agitation against the British Government in the form of Civil Disobedience, and Non-Cooperation movements. Straddling the movement in the middle between the two extremities of the spectrum stood those who adopted the old-school **Gokhale-Ranade** methods of "*gradualism*" that sought freedom from the British by pressing home their advantage not through overly agitational or revolutionary methods but by exploiting the imperial Britain's own inherent sense of justice and fair-play, "*constitutionalism*" and much-touted "*liberal-humanist*" (Fabian social-democracy) values and "*civilisational ethics*".

**** ****

Srinivasa Sastri belonged to this third group. Although he and Gandhi differed in their choice and paths of political activism --- in that classic moral binary where the *End clashes with Means* -- the astute judge of men's innate talents that Mahatma Gandhi was made him recognize and skilfully commission and deploy Sastri's many versatile skills and capabilities to further his own goals.

Gandhi returned for good to India in the early 1920s after having spent many years working for the rights and freedoms of the indentured Indian community there. It was in South Africa that his "*experiments with truth*" and the methods of "***satyagraha***" had been put into practise and then honed and developed into a powerful weapon of non-violent political agitation. Gandhi was all set then to unleash that weapon in India too against British Imperial rule and for Independence.

The British Government in India was acutely aware of the danger of Gandhi's *Satyagraha* mass-movement stratagem getting exported from India to South Africa and fomenting there in that country the same *Civil Disobedience and Non-Cooperation* movements which were gathering steam at home under the auspices of the Gandhi-led **Indian National Congress**. The virus of *Satyagraha*, the British were convinced, if it did spread to South Africa too, it would very likely lead to a sort of cross-border *consolidation or coalition of freedom-fighters* in India and South African Indians. That would cause a potential cross-continental political crisis for the British Crown that was already tottering from the ravages of the First World War and gradually but inevitably lurching towards the Second one at that time.

Gandhi was acutely aware of the many deep dangers of such a virus spreading from colonial India to colonial South Africa. Although sympathetic to the almost slavish condition of the Indian community in Durban, Natal and Pretoria provinces that the emerging apartheid regime in South Africa had ruthlessly imposed upon it, Gandhi nonetheless realised that that the general demographic, political and social environment of South Africa were not the same as in India.

With intimate, first-hand knowledge of the South African Indian-community gained during his years when he practised as an activist-lawyer there, Gandhi knew that the community was not yet ready for mass *Satyagraha* movement. It would be too early and too potentially self-destructive for Indians in South Africa to confront and take head-on the might of British Rule by resorting to methods that Gandhi had launched and set in motion at home in India. The reason why he felt so was because of the poor level and standards of education and social awareness amongst them of law, constitution, political and civil rights.

Also, Gandhi's own unerring sense of the unpredictable trajectories that mass political movements could take to lead towards unforeseen consequences warned him that if a crisis were to explode amongst Indians in South Africa, it was sure to severely affect the course, the momentum and the prospects of success of India's own freedom struggles at home against the British.

So, under such overarching circumstances, Gandhi and the ***Indian National Congress (INC)*** were compelled to tacitly support the British Crown and its Government in India in efforts to put a tight lid on -- and contain -- any potential political movements for freedom such as mass *Satyagraha* or *Civil Unrest* breaking out in South Africa.

*** ***

The British thus used very ingenious diplomacy to persuade Gandhi and INC to be and serve them as a sort of *"ambassadors-at-large"* in South Africa to dissuade the Indian community from pursuing any sort of political activism against British Rule and, instead, focus more on the greater goal of amelioration of its overall social, educational and economic plight.

Thus, did the leadership of the INC enter a sort of unwritten pact under which Gandhi would himself undertake to carry out the very delicate diplomatic and international task of mediation and conciliation between the Crown and its Indian subjects in South Africa.

To put the entire matter in broad historical perspective and to describe in a nutshell exactly what the British Government of India did, one may use the Tamil idiom: **"முள்ளை கொண்டு முள்ளை எடுத்தல்"** (*"Mullai kondu mullai eduththal"*). In other words, the delicate diplomacy the British used to diffuse or defuse the potentially crisis-situation likely to break out in South Africa was to skilfully enlist the Mahatma himself to handle the assignment of persuading the Indian community to forsake -- at least for the time being then -- any idea or program of freedom struggle against the British being contemplated and instead to focus more on its own economic betterment and social development.

Mahatma Gandhi was caught in a bind. On one hand, he knew he had no choice but to accede to the British Government's wishes. On the other hand, he also knew that he himself could not go to South Africa to carry out the diplomatic mission since he and the INC were already committed to the freedom struggle movement in India. If he left India to return to South Africa it would severely cripple and compromise the freedom struggle the INC was waging against the British at home.

Gandhi thus looked around for a workaround and it was then that he immediately recognized that the job of carrying out such delicate international diplomacy entrusted to him by the Colonial Rulers had to be delegated to someone admirably qualified for it. And Gandhi did not have to look too far and wide in India to recruit such a person.

It had to be the eminent **Srinivasa Sastri***!*

Gandhi thus put aside all his ideological differences with Sastri and persuaded him to take up the assignment to go to Durban as the emissary *de jure* of not only the Government of India but *de facto*, as his very own personal one!

**** ****

Gandhi's insistence that Sastri go to South Africa to represent Indian interests abroad highlights how Gandhi valued Sastri's stature and language skills as critical assets in international advocacy. Gandhi's political strategy increasingly began incorporating those assets in making appeals to British public opinion and international bodies.

Sastri's role symbolized this strategy of engaging colonial authorities through persuasion and legal arguments, complementing Gandhi's mass mobilization at home. The letter that was written on **April 6, 1927,** thus indeed shows Gandhi's recognition of Sastri's personal integrity, educational background, and ability to act as an interpreter or mediator. Gandhi's approach often involved aligning himself with respected intellectual figures like Sastri to lend moral and intellectual weight to the independence movement, balancing popular street-level Satyagraha agitation with respectable leadership.

Sastri was known for his deep knowledge of constitutional law, diplomacy, and his eloquence in English. Gandhi's letter reflects respect for Sastri's calm, reasoned approach and his ability to represent Indian interests effectively in official and international settings. This influenced Gandhi's strategic use of constitutional dialogue alongside mass civil disobedience, balancing confrontation with negotiation. It was no surprise that Gandhi's choice of Sastri to be the man for the assignment was influenced by Gandhi knowing coming to know only too well that Sastri respected constitutionalism, diplomacy, and the importance of international advocacy within the Indian independence movement.

Sastri's intellectual rigor and polished public persona thus would only complement Gandhi's mass-based activism, leading to a multi-pronged political strategy that combined moral suasion with direct action.

There can be no doubt thus that it was Srinivasa Sastri who indeed did help Gandhi to broaden the nationalist movement's reach and impact during the critical phases of the freedom struggle in the 1920-early 1930s.

**** ****

In South Africa, Srinivasa Sastry handled the truly unenviable task of walking an extremely tight rope of diplomacy, having to represent both the British Imperial Government of India as well as Mahatma Gandhi and furthermore, at the same time, also work to advance the interests of the Indian community at large.

Sastri was acutely aware of the perilous assignment he was about to carry out. He was sent to South Africa to act as bridge between a disenfranchised, disempowered, impoverished Indian community and the British Colonial Establishment.

The Indians were disenchanted with the same Colonial Rulers whose representative, ironically, Sastri was! He was also acutely aware that the Indian community would be only to easily prone to compare and pass judgment upon the work he did for them and their causes with the sterling work they had in earlier years witnessed Mahatma Gandhi accomplish.

In a very candid speech that he made to a gathering of Indians in Durban, Sastri was not afraid to be open and honest in laying bare the precarious nature of his assignment:

I will speak about my own mission. As you are aware, I am the first official representative of India in this sub-continent. What led to the creation of the office is within the full experience and knowledge of nearly all of you. But I may be allowed to take you behind the Cape Town Agreement, just to dwell for a moment on the anxieties and fears with which the Government of India and the Imperial Cabinet of Great Britain had always viewed the situation created by the circumstances in which Indians were living in this country, and generally in the Dominions of Britain abroad.

I do not wish to say anything that may be unpleasant or anything that may be in the nature of recrimination. My purpose is not to make matters worse but to make them better, and if I recall the condition and anxieties and fears prevalent among the Government and the people in one common state. If I dwell upon this aspect of the subject, it is merely to show that the Government of India, in handling an extremely difficult and delicate situation, have thought it their duty, first and foremost, to avoid anything that may be in the nature of a diplomatic blunder; for **diplomatic blunders have consequences that are far reaching, and fall, in the main, on**

innocent people and upon generations who are perfectly innocent of the complications through which they are made to suffer.

As representative of the Government of India, it behoves me, also, to walk warily where there are so many pitfalls, and to avoid anything which may be in the nature of added bitterness, for bitterness there is in abundance in all conscience, and if one desires to cure one cannot start by making the disease worse.

As it turned out, during the two odd, staggered years that Srinivasa Sastri spent in South Africa -- first when he arrived there in **December 1926** as a member of the *Habibullah Delegation* which was sent from India to negotiate and study the position and grievances of the Indian community living there. The delegation was officially led by *Sir Mohammad Habibullah*, a member of the Viceroy's *Executive Council*. The delegation was organized after rising tensions and discriminatory laws against Indians were passed in South Africa, notably policies restricting Indian immigration and civil rights. Its purpose was to conduct on-the-ground investigations, negotiate with South African authorities, and seek a diplomatic solution to the discrimination faced by the Indian minority, without explicitly endorsing *"repatriation"* (return of Indians to India), which South Africa favoured.

Although led by Habibullah in title, V. S. Srinivasa Sastri emerged as the main spokesperson and negotiator for Indian interests during the mission, owing to his diplomatic skill and reputation.

Then again when Sastri returned to South Africa in **June 1927** to work as the **Agent-General to the Government of India** until **January 1929**), the work he did for the Indian Community and for the British Crown earned him effusive encomiums from both!

How did Sastri pull it off?

**** **** ****

Chapter 3
The "*method of inoffensive kindliness*"

The diplomatic tight-rope walking that **Rt. Hon'ble Srinivasa Sastri** had to execute in his remit as the *Agent-General of the Imperial Government of India (1927-29)* in South Africa was accomplished not only with great dexterity but also aplomb. For the services he rendered to both the British Government as well as to the Indian community at large in South Africa, and within such a short span of time, he earned fulsome praise and gratitude.

In 1931 -- as much as we see today in 2025 in the **Sastri School**'s plans for commemorating 2029 as their centenary year in Durban -- South Africans remembered Srinivasa Sastri with great affection even two long years after he had left them to return to India. Such was the undying admiration and respect he aroused in South Africans. Below was a heartfelt tribute in 1931 penned by two South Africans of India-origin:

"*Mr. Sastri returned us the first Agent General to the Government of India in the Union in June 1927. He sailed for India on January 28, 1929. His stay in the country was eighteen months first for a year, and, on the request of the Governor-General of South Africa (**the Earl of Athlone**) and the Viceroy of India (**Lord Irwin**), he agreed to remain for a further period of six months.*

"*What eighteen months they were! A veritable king commanding homage wherever he went, winning over opposition and working unremittingly and persevering in labour for the advancement of the community. Now and again, he would feel the burden of overwork, the infirmities of the body and the pain of advancing years, and for the moment he would lift aside the veil to those in close touch with him who might share in his disappointments.*

“"Oh, if I were young!"” he once said to us, “"It is a work which demands youth, in its vision and optimism to help in bringing about a state of the South African Indian acceptable to the country, an enlightened community that any people will be proud to claim its own. I am now old, weak in strength and the power to do. It was the will of the people of India that I came. Had it only been

a few years ago! I wish for strength so that I can move about from one end of the country to the other, wherever a solitary Indian is to be found, sounding a clarion call to duty to this his country of domicile and birth.""

"Despite what he felt to be his limitations, very few would assert that he failed. If, he maintained, the British Commonwealth was based on equity to the least among its fellows, then the Europeans of South Africa, who were assured of the dominance of Western civilisation, must concede the right of the Indian to a proper place in the country. Mr. Sastri's pleadings for the recognition of this aspect rose to heights of eloquence unsurpassed and unrivalled.

"Urging this plea with moderation and forbearance, he won to the cause he served the unqualified friendship and co-operation of the best of both the white races, Dutch and British. There are many amongst us who may still recall his speeches, combined with wonderful diction and thought; and ere the echo of the silvery cadence die, the figure grow dim, and the appeal lose its force, may we be permitted to preserve, even in its imperfections, the words of that great Indian-- Srinivasa Sastri who may yet speak to us and the succeeding generations. (**S.R. Naidoo and Dhanee Bramdaw - 1931**)

**** ****

Neither Mahatma Gandhi nor the British Imperial Government could have ever found anyone else in India to serve as equal if not a better Ambassador in South Africa than Srinivasa Sastri. For, he excelled not only as a consummate and suave diplomat but also in the capacity of an extraordinary cultural exemplar of Indian civilisation. Another South African, a *white man*, wrote this about him:

"Not often does one find a speaker who at once has something to say, which is so well worth saying, and is able to say it with such distinction and such charm."

"Of the significance of Mr. Sastri's ambassadorship for the Indians in South Africa it is hardly for me to speak; but one need not go beyond the speeches .... to find evidence of his wisdom in counsel, his discretion, his understanding sympathy, his unerring statesmanship."

"To the Europeans of our land his sojourn in our midst meant perhaps more than anything else the presentation of a new conception of India and its people. He became to us the interpreter of India--- an India of which, to our shame be

it said, we used to know all too little; or, where we knew of it, we allowed, all too readily, our remembrance of it to be obscured."

"He revealed to us an India of an ancient civilisation, one of the great civilisations of the world, a civilisation which has made many important contributions to our modern life; an India of a serene philosophy, a wide culture, and a developed art; an India with a literature well worthy to be numbered among the great literatures of the world. **Of that India we did not know before Mr. Sastri came among us or, if we knew of it, we did not often think of it.** *He made it real to us, and against the background which he thus created,* **he made it possible for us to see what we have called our Indian problem in a different way."**

"Fortunate indeed was India when she sent Mr. Sastri as her interpreter to South Africa. But Mr. Sastri did more than reveal India to South Africa. **He also, in his own inimitable way, did much to reveal us to ourselves, helping us to see—no less effectively because of the kindly inoffensiveness of the method** *-- some of those things wherein we are in danger as a nation of falling short of those high principles to which we owe allegiance."* **(Jan H. Hofmeyer 1930)**

**** ****

1. How did Sastri succeed in not only "*revealing India to South Africa*" but as South Africans themselves felt, he "*also, in his own inimitable way, did much to reveal us to ourselves?*"

2. What was Sastri's ***"method of kindly inoffensiveness"*** that made the British Colonial Rulers of South Africa realise that they were "*... in danger as a nation of falling short of those high principles to which we owe allegiance?*"

3. And what was that tremendous work which Sastri said had demanded "*a vision and optimism to help in bringing about a state of the South African Indian acceptable to the country, an enlightened community that any people will be proud to claim its own?*"

Sastri's *"method of kindly offensiveness"* was employed in his diplomacy when he appealed to the higher, nobler nature and human instincts of Imperial Rulers. It also included his sage advice to the Indian community in South Africa to eschew any form of revolutionary confrontation with the Imperial State for the sake of their immediate and long-term interests. Like the good old schoolteacher and headmaster that Sastri was in personal disposition and political predilection, he urged South African Indians to instead concentrate on the priority of *Educating* themselves, their children and women since that was the key indeed to economic and social development.

Sastri's "*method of kindly inoffensiveness*" was nowhere more well and convincingly demonstrated than in his splendid public speeches that were on occasions addressed both to the Imperial Rulers there, indirectly, as well as directly to the Indian community.

Sastri held up a large mirror, as it were, to the face of British Colonialism so that its Rulers in South Africa could get a good look at themselves in it and, in good conscience, realise their duty and obligations to their subjects; and having thereby to justify even to themselves that they were truly what they claimed to be: a supreme but civilised race and an imperial power in the world that was a force for the good. Sastri asked them:

" Would you be justified in ordering the lives of Indians amongst you?

"Would you be justified in ordering their lives in going further than might be necessary in order to secure this essential condition?

"Would it be wise; would it be in accordance with the highest civilised rules; would it be in conformity with the highest standard set up by Great Britain in various parts of the Empire? Would it be right to raise bars and barriers which are not necessary to maintain your supremacy, but which seem only designed to deny the Indian, sometimes wholly, sometimes partially, the opportunities and facilities which are necessary for his full development? He has no right to shape your politics or alter institutions to his own benefit. But is it necessary (for you) to bind him with shackles and fetters which deprive him of the opportunities to which, as a citizen of the British Empire, as one who swears allegiance to the Throne of Great Britain, he is entitled? Is it

necessary to impose limitations on him as to the profession he might follow, or on the education he might wish to receive?"

"Is it or is it not a part of the aims of every civilised Government that every citizen, except he be of evil character or disloyal conduct, shall be allowed to become himself fully? I believe that the ordinary canons of right and justice will give the answer, without reservation, in the affirmative to that question.

There is the promise held out by the Sovereign of Great Britain on dozens of public solemn occasions. There is the course consistently held by a long period of Imperial rule by Great Britain, a course which will not be deviated by a hair's breadth, which require that no one will be denied that which is necessary for developing himself.

"Whether the institutions are monarchical, oligarchic or democratic, no matter which shape they may assume in outward form, their tendency must always be to utilise all the available talent in the country to the fullest advantage not only for one section, because it may be dominant, but for the whole community. Every one of the communities is interested not only in giving the best to the whole collectively of the State but he is interested in exacting from the rest of the community the best possible for that collectivity.

" **"Equal rights for every civilised man"** *is the motto of administration which on all occasions has (to be) followed. It is my fervent prayer that nothing will tempt you to depart from the straight and broad path.*

"The Government of India wishes nothing better than that they (the British) shall adhere to this formula in all that they do with reference to the Indian people. I have neither the knowledge nor the experience to answer the question which may be put: "What are the signs of contemporary time, is that formula in jeopardy, what are the currents of opinion that might wreck that formula ...? I put the question, but the answer must come from those whose daily lives have been spent in studying the details and the tendencies of administration."

"As one who wishes with all my heart that the British Commonwealth will continue for a long, long time yet in the history of the world to be the exemplar of the highest principles of rule, to be the pattern of all that is best, to secure the welfare of human kind, I pray you not to deviate from the high standard set up by (Cecil) Rhodes, while you might be absolutely required to keep your own supremacy and maintain your own traditions, but to ask the other Provinces to

come along and take their stand on your side as the custodians of even-handed justice and fair play, to maintain the high level of British justice, British equity and the British desire to give every individual under the common flag an opportunity."

"*I can assist my countrymen only by assisting you.*"

**** ****

The "*method of inoffensive kindliness*" of Srinivasa Sastri also got gently blended into his style of diplomacy while dealing with the Indian community in South Africa. He *inoffensively* chided them on grossly neglecting their education and the schooling of their children. He told them this in a speech:

"*To the Indian (community), I say do not misjudge me; I have not come here to exalt myself in the eyes of the Europeans at your expense. But you have always to remember that you cannot ask anything until you have established fully your desire to benefit by it. I visited the Indian School, and I was sad to see the small number in the higher hall.*

Allow your children to have all the facilities of education that are offered to them. I know how you love your children. But every true father desires nothing more than that he should be excelled and (sur)passed by his son. I would rather prefer you to be beggars wandering from door to door than that you should have abundance to eat and leave your children in ignorance. It is wrong to take away children from school after the fourth standard. It seems to me that you should have protection up to 17 or 18 years of age. And you should pay even greater attention to the education of your girls. You can only neglect the careful education of your girls at the peril of the community.

**** ****

When after 1929 Sastri had returned to India having accomplished the task that had been assigned to him by Gandhi and the British Government, did he receive the same appreciation and accolades from his own compatriots and colleagues in the *Indian National Congress* that the grateful South African Indian community in Durban and elsewhere had thought it fit to shower upon him?

**** **** ****

Chapter 4
Anglophilia and "mute submission"

By the time Srinivasa Sastri returned in 1929 to India after successfully completing the diplomatic task in South Africa that had been assigned to him by the British Government of India and by Mahatma Gandhi as well, his intellectual and political stature had grown tremendously and he became renowned amongst both the Colonial Administrations of Great Britain and South Africa and as well as in the wider Indian political spheres at home.

Srinivasa Sastri, due to his wide-ranging erudition, strong affinity with and remarkable command of the English language, his polished oratory style, and his constitutional approach of moderation that inclined towards cooperation with the British rather than confrontation had already gained considerable fame worldwide. He was admired by many British leaders and intellectuals for his eloquence—**King George V** made him a "*Companion of Honour,*" and British Prime Ministers and historians praised his English oratory highly.

However, within the political circles in India -- at that time in the 1930s when Gandhi's *Civil Disobedience Movement* and *Satyagraha* mass-agitations were gathering enormous momentum thanks to a rising tide of nation-wide nationalism – Sastri was not admired by the leadership of the **Indian National Congress** even half as much as those in the vaulting corridors of imperial power in Whitehall, Westminster in London. Despite the personal rapport and trust that Sastri enjoyed with Mahatma Gandhi, he found himself terribly at odds with the likes of Jawaharlal Nehru, Sardar Patel, Rajaji and other stalwarts of the Congress Party.

Srinivasa Sastri had earlier, in fact, himself held positions in the *Indian National Congress*! He had joined the Congress in 1908 and had served as the *Secretary of the Madras District Congress Committee* in 1911. He had been quite an active member until 1922 when he resigned in protest against the **Non-Cooperation Movement** initiated by Gandhi and the Congress leadership. Sastri viewed the movement as radical and extra-constitutional. He doubted the ability of Gandhi's followers and apostles to maintain pacifism and was critical of the confrontational approach, preferring constitutional methods and cooperation with the British colonial framework.

During his time with the Congress, Sastri came to be known for his moderate but staunchly constitutional approach to the struggle for independence. It inevitably led to a falling out with the more radical *"top brass"* (high command) of the *Indian National Congress* headed by Jawaharlal Nehru, Sardar Patel, and C. Rajagopalachari (Rajaji).

Sastri resigned from the Congress.

**** ****

After leaving the Congress, Srinivasa Sastri went on to found the **Indian Liberal Federation** (or *Indian Liberal Party*). He was content to continue his political work through that platform which represented a less popular but far more moderate, liberal, and constitutionalist segment within Indian politics, distinct from the mass civil disobedience and radical nationalist strategies pursued by the Congress leadership.

In spite of Sastri having repudiated the INC and leaving it, the fact that Mahatma Gandhi had still handpicked him and had also wholly endorsed the British Government's choice of his candidacy to go to South Africa as *Agent-General* on an important ambassadorial assignment, (it is my surmise that it) may have caused considerable pique – or envy or both -

- against him amongst the "*top brass*" of the Congress. To further add to the consternation of Nehru and other leaders of the INC, Srinivasa Sastri was also nominated to join the important **Delegation of prominent Indian leaders** attending -- in **1930-32** -- the historic **Round Table Conferences** in London.

These lengthy Conferences were held to deliberate upon and make recommendations for *Constitutional Reforms* related to British Rule in India which did, in fact, have far-reaching ramifications later in history for the Independence of India.

At these crucial meetings of the *Round Table* convened by the British Government in London, Sastri participated actively while making significant contributions to the proceedings. But then he did so not on behalf of the *Indian National Congress* but as the leader of the *Indian Liberal Federation.* The inputs and recommendations given by him at the Conferences were at complete variance with those of the INC's own approach and strategies. Thus, the "*top brass*" of the Congress Party became even more resentful and deeply critical than before of Srinivasa Sastri.

Nehru's worst suspicions about Sastri's ideological stance *vis-a-vis* how the Freedom Struggle against the British must be conducted were confirmed. He was irked deeply by Sastri's steadfast view that the struggle for India's Independence must be based firmly on principles of "*constitutionalism*" and not upon the fervour of "*nationalism*". Nehru felt that Sastri was overly sympathetic to and cooperative with the British rulers, as the record of his work in South Africa had already shown and then, also especially evident at the *Round Table Conferences* where Sastri and his associates had largely accepted British proposals that the Congress itself had rejected as unfair.

Sastri's stance favoured *dominion status for British India* and ongoing *constitutional reform* over *immediate full independence.* This position put him, ideologically, squarely apart from the Congress mainstream led by Nehru, Patel, and Rajaji. The mainstream INC thus became hostile towards Sastri. It began an imperceptible yet strident campaign of criticism against Srinivasa Sastri despite his being in the good books of Mahatma Gandhi. Their criticism was aimed at what was perceived as Sastri's excessive sympathy for and cooperation with British colonial rulers. Nehru saw Sastri as too conciliatory and cooperative with the British, especially during moments of crisis and political struggle. For example, Nehru remarked in his ***Autobiography*** that although *"Sastri was an excellent orator"*, he advocated ***"mute submission"*** to the British and was *"not very effective"* during critical times when followers needed strong leadership.

**** ****

It is quite probable that apart from ideological difference of opinion, Nehru's distinct discomfort with Sastri arose also from a suppressed sense of envy.

In the 1930s, Jawaharlal Nehru was unquestionably the rising star within the *Indian National Congress.* He commanded the awe and obedience of the entire Party rank and file. He was indeed the *Crown Prince*, the undeclared *heir to the Mahatma.* And Nehru was respected in the country also for his comprehensive and unmatched grasp of world affairs, international relations and diplomacy. Handling *foreign affairs* was considered Nehru's turf and forte and none within the INC could dare challenge him on that front. If at all there was any Indian at that time who could easily hold a candle to Jawaharlal Nehru if not perhaps even excel him, it could be none other than the Rt. Hon'ble Srinivasa Sastri.

Sastri's mastery of the English language, polished oratory, and constitutional approach made him an elite diplomat and international representative of Indian interests. He had shown that he could successfully engage with British political leaders and that too with great aplomb even at august global forums like the *League of Nations, the Imperial Conference*, and diplomatic missions to South Africa and the UK. His diplomatic efforts, such as the forging of the *Cape Town Agreement* with South Africa in safeguarding Indian minority rights, were truly pioneering, as it represented India in a very sophisticated light within the international liberal framework.

Sastri's work also had helped advance Indian self-respect globally and it laid the groundwork for India's evolving global legitimacy, moving toward the idea of dominion status within the British Empire. Here was a man then who -- quite like Nehru himself -- thus took to international diplomacy and India's *Foreign Affairs* like duck to water. Nehru the rising star in the INC, thus, could not have relished Sastri being looked upon as an equal expert on foreign affairs. That title, many Congressmen believed, belonged exclusively to Nehru, and so he would brook no challengers.

Above all, what might have also irritated Nehru no end was the fact that Mahatma Gandhi himself personally valued Sastri's role for presenting Indian claims in global fora, complementing thereby Gandhi's mass civil disobedience with Sastri's constitutional diplomacy and intellectual weight.

Nehru thus, it can be reasonably conjectured, had much personal motive indeed to grow quite hypercritical of what he believed was Sastri's *diplomatic elitism* and *caste/racial biases* which, in fact, he charged, were what had distanced Sastri, in the first place, from the mass movements of the INC and had also alienated him from the vast population of poor, marginalized Indians.

Within the INC rank and file in some quarters, a conspiratorial narrative eventually thus gained currency and began circulating in hushed whispers and murmurs: Sastri's diplomacy often reflected *elitism* and a kind of "*performative Brahminess*" emphasizing refined Indian culture and very much distanced from poorer Indians and indigenous allies. And furthermore, that Sastri's kind of elitism in the country was what was weakening mass movements and *Satyagraha* for India's political rights. The narrative also falsely described Sastri's efforts to separate Indian concerns from those of other marginalized groups like *black South Africans* during his diplomatic work as very problematic, and that it only concealed his own deep caste and racial biases which could only limit solidarity and broader nationalist appeal.

All the above points were clearly reflected in Nehru's remarks about Sastri in his *Autobiography* and elsewhere in episodic instances.

**** ****

It is important for us today who are students of history to clearly understand what *Anglophilia* meant at the time in the history of the Indian Independence struggle.

Anglophile elites, typically Western-educated middle-class professionals (*lawyers, teachers, journalists, academicians who came from the Brahmin caste*), played a major role in introducing constitutional, legal, and diplomatic methods to the independence cause. Their familiarity with British political institutions enabled them to negotiate with colonial authorities and represent Indian interests internationally. Their engagement helped frame Indian nationalism within a global legal and diplomatic context, advancing Indian claims through constitutional reforms, dialogue, and international forums.

Leaders like Srinivasa Sastri exemplified this trait that was contemptuously called *Anglophilia* because he was adept in using mastery of English and British-style diplomacy to advocate for Indian rights abroad, complementing mass movements led by figures such as Gandhi.

Leaders like Nehru -- despite being himself an unabashed *Anglophile* in every sense of the term -- adopted a posture of being very allergic to so-called "*Anglophilia*" in others like Sastri only because it suited them politically to neutralise those whom they saw as ideological rivals. The best way to do that was to accuse leaders like Sastri of turning into elitist toadies of the British. The elites' focus on *constitutionalism*, Congressmen cleverly argued, sometimes did slow or complicate more confrontational efforts in the freedom struggle, leading thus to internal disagreements, within the freedom struggle movement, over broad strategy.

Nonetheless, Mahatma Gandhi, at least, very clearly understood that the so-called "*anglophile elites*" of India were contributing very essential diplomatic skills, constitutional knowledge, and international legitimacy to India's independence struggle through their advocation of moderation and cooperation with British institutions. Their dual role in a way helped him shape a pluralistic nationalist movement balancing *elite negotiation* and *mass resistance* simultaneously, although their perceived affinity with British interests sometimes limited their influence among radical nationalists.

**** ****

Due to such a surreptitious or snide campaign of calumny unleashed by the top leadership of the *Indian National Congress* against him, Srinivasa Sastri soon came to be branded in mainstream Indian politics as an

Anglophile. And to add insult to injury, he was also disdained as a "***performative orthodox Brahmin***".

How and why did such blatantly unfair stereotyping of Sastri happen?

It would require the forensic skills of a professional historian delving into that specific period in history to study it and be able to write about how exactly it happened. But it would not be unreasonable to surmise here (for me) that Srinivasa Sastri got stuck with that unsavoury tag of *"elite Anglophile"* thanks mainly to misunderstanding and grossly misinterpreting -- by ripping everything out of context -- many of his public utterances... especially the eloquent speeches he had given in South Africa, which was where he had achieved the most impactful work in his career as a gentleman-diplomat.

Here below is just one sample of such a speech Sastri had gone on record to have made (in 1927) and the likes of which, most probably, served later as damning grist and evidence for the rumour mills of Delhi that were spreading malicious canards about Sastri's *Anglophilia*, and which Congressmen came to believe was true.

"It is no part of our intention either now or at any time in the future to challenge the political supremacy of the white part of the population of South Africa. We admit to the full your right to maintain the civilisation which you value, the modes of living, the standards of comfort which you have set up for yourselves, amidst discouragement and difficulties, which we fully appreciate. We recognise that it will be your right to determine the public policy of this sub-continent, and model it to yours and the satisfaction of the public interests."

"This being out of the way, we recognise as a natural corollary that there must be certain limitations and restrictions upon the political and municipal freedom of Indians here (in South Africa) so that this essential requirement may be satisfied. We are anxious to disarm your suspicions in the matter."

"And any application which might be made for the freedom of the Indian population in a request for the removal of disabilities pressing upon them, and any petition for facilities enabling them to live a happy, contented and prosperous life—all these things must be understood as being subject to this limitation, with which no wish is there to interfere in, or dispute the political supremacy of, the Europeans of this sub-continent."

**** ****

Anyone today reading the above extract of Sastri's speech without any knowledge of the real context in which it was made in South Africa at that time might unthinkingly only jump to the conclusion that *yes,* as Nehru had accused him, Sastri must have been, "*overly sympathetic and cooperative with the British rulers*" and that "*he seemed to advocate" mute submission"* to them.

To the best of my knowledge, there is little that is on record in the public domain reporting that Rt. Hon'ble Srinivasa Sastri ever defended himself against the accusation of "*elitist toadyism*" hurled against him. He would never have stooped to that level of countering uncharitable slander whispered about him behind his back... He would simply have ignored it all and withdrawn into hurt silence. To defend himself under such circumstances in the newspapers or in the public square would have been beneath the man who was known always for having maintained the dignity of his *"method of kindly inoffensiveness"*.

There is a very emotional passage in the very same speech of Sastri quoted above. It was made in South Africa on an entirely different occasion. But in my view, those could be the very words that Sastri might have repeated to us if he were he to be called today by us to offer an explanation, a justification or a defence of what he was charged with by peers and rivals in politics back in 1930-32. And those words in his own defence would surely qualify yet as another classic example of his "*method of kindly inoffensiveness:*"

"*You know, being men and women of the world, that there is only one truth and a thousand lies; there is only one course of action in a difficulty and there are beside it a hundred wrong courses each inviting you to itself. It is hard—I realise it fully-- it is hard to do what is right, to speak the truth, to keep to the straight path in front of you when there are temptations to make a great mark, to create a sensation which the superficial observer will regard as smart or clever, but which cannot contribute anything to remove the evil of the situation."*

"*Suspicions had been aroused, accusations had been flung about recklessly, that it is necessary to be quite clear and emphatic on the point. It is, unfortunately, true, in the political world, that when politicians repudiate something, we usually suppose that there is something wrong about it. Politicians are a tribe who do not always trust one another. When they repudiate anything, they are anxious that the repudiation shall be taken at its face value, that their honesty shall not be questioned, and their bona fides shall be above cavil. But, when another man repudiates anything, they laugh, ignore it, even sneer and say, "We know what these political statements are!"*

*"I want you to acquit me of saying anything that will look like a political statement of this kind. There cannot be any temptation for me to deceive you in making a statement in which I did not fully believe. I have a sacred duty to the cause I represent. There are circumstances surrounding my work; there is sufficient guarantee that I will not make myself consciously guilty of exaggeration, a wilful distortion of the facts or a calculated concealment of feelings deep in the mi*nd."

**** ****

After the *"unkindly offensive"* way in which he was treated by the leadership of the *Indian National Congress,* Srinivasa Sastri political career began to unravel and rapidly wane... He became slowly a broken man.... How did he cope with the isolation? To what did he turn his attention next in life?

**** **** ****

Chapter 5
Brothers-in-Arms: Gandhi and Sastri

Between his return to India from South Africa in 1939 until his death in 1946, how did Sastri occupy himself? What were his major political accomplishments and contributions to the Freedom movement? And what were his other pursuits, literary and academic?

Between 1939 and 1946, Sastri's life was devoted to literary scholarship, educational leadership, and the pursuit of a constitutional, united India. Though marginalized politically by the ascendant radical nationalists of the INC under Nehru, Patel, Rajaji and others, he continued to shape debates on *education, language policy, national identity, and communal unity.* His substantial body of *literary work—autobiographical, biographical, and interpretive*—combined with his commitment to *public service*, represents his enduring legacy in Indian political and cultural life.

It would be superfluous here (for me) to recount what History already and abundantly has recorded as Sastri's many contributions in the above-mentioned spheres of public life. So, merely a brief listing ... i.e. a *montage...* of the most significant of them is all that is given below so that as students of Indian history we can all jog our memories of it while also, at the same time, revisit some important chapters in the life-history of Srinivasa Sastri.

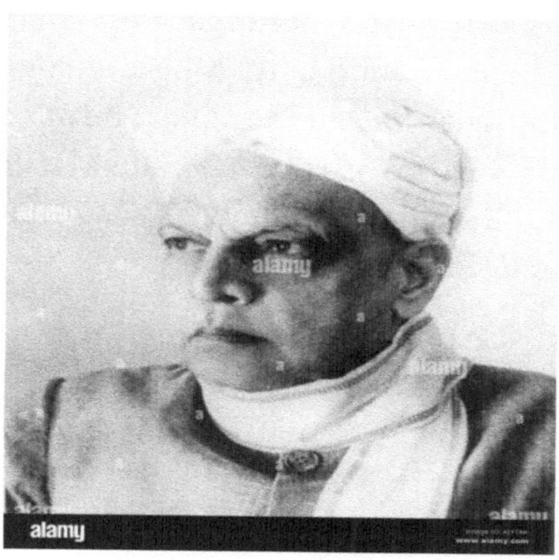

1. **Public and Political Roles**

a) **Advocacy and Liberal Federation:** Sastri continued to lead and guide the *Indian Liberal Federation*, advocating constitutional approaches, dominion status, and communal harmony. He became a key voice against the partition of India, expressing strong opposition to the ***Muslim League's*** demands for the division of the country.

b) **Appeal for Dominion Status:** During World War II, he was part of a multi-party Indian delegation urging Prime Minister Winston Churchill to grant India dominion status, in recognition of India's support to the Allies.

c) **Opposition to Partition:** In his final years, Sastri was a leading voice opposing the partition of India, emphasizing secular constitutionalism and national unity.

d) **Support for Constitutional Reform:** He promoted peaceful, negotiated constitutional advancement toward full self-government, a stand that, although overshadowed by more radical movements, influenced moderate and intellectual circles.

e) **Advisor and Public Intellectual:** Sastri often advised both government and political leaders, using his diplomatic experience to influence debates, especially around minority protections and communal relations.

2. **Educational and Literary Work.**

a) **Language Policy and Translation:** In 1940, the Madras government appointed Sastri to head a committee tasked with standardizing scientific and technical terminology in Tamil. His recommendation—**to retain Sanskrit-derived words—** sparked the first major Tamil language policy debate in the *Madras Presidency.*

b) **University Leadership:** Up to 1940, Sastri was **Vice Chancellor of Annamalai University,** and he remained involved in educational matters with an emphasis on Indian values and modernity.

c) **Scholar, Orator, and Literary Figure:** During this period, Sastri focused on writing, reviewing, and translating key historical and literary texts. He was famed as an orator and writer in both English and Tamil and continued to publish essays and lectures.

d) **Autobiographical and Reflective Essays:** Sastri's autobiographical essays in Tamil, most notably compiled as **'மீண்டும் வாழ்ந்தால்'** (*Meendum Vazhndhaal, "If I Live Again,"* 1944), reflect his personal philosophy, national ideals, and struggles.

- **(i) Historical and Biographical Works:** He wrote biographies of eminent personalities—such as *"Life and Times of Sir Pherozeshah Mehta"* (1945), *"My Master Gokhale"* (published posthumously in 1946), and *"Life of Gopala Krishna Gokhale"* (1937) — that remain valued for their insight and literary grace.
- **(ii) Translation and Scholarship:** Sastri condensed and interpreted the **"Valmiki Ramayana" (1935)**, promoted appreciation of Indian and world classics, and contributed essays on his literary influences.
- **(iii) Reviewing Gandhi's Works:** He proofread and corrected the manuscript of Gandhi's autobiography, ***"The Story of My Experiments with Truth,"*** and reviewed successive issues of Gandhi's magazine *"Harijan"*.

3. **Intellectual Legacy:** Even as political currents in India in the 1930s and 1940s marginalized moderates of his generation, Sastri's voice was respected for its erudition, moral force, and literary craft—he was seen as *India's premier liberal constitutionalist* and a model for statesmanlike public discourse. In fact, long before the idea of an **Indian Constitution** crystallized itself after 1947 -- and which lay dormant as something referred to as an obscure, musty *"White Paper"* within the *Indian National Congress* office at that time -- Srinivasa Sastri was already engaged in serious and very lively conversations about it with Mahatma Gandhi during1932-33.

4. **Death:** Sastri died in Madras (now Chennai) on **17 April 1946** after a period of declining health.

**** ****

It was during the above period i.e. between 1930 when he returned from South Africa to India and 1946 when he passed away, that Srinivasa Sastri, though imperceptibly but unequivocally marginalised by the political coteries surrounding Jawaharlal Nehru, nonetheless maintained very intimate and endearing personal relations with Mahatma Gandhi.

Gandhi, born on ***October 2,*** and Sastri born on ***September 22*** of the same year in **1869 CE,** was a mere fortnight Sastri's junior by age. Throughout those decades, the two of them exchanged scores of personal, private letters with each other, discussing dozens of issues and affairs related to the Freedom struggle and a host of social issues like *Harijan welfare, Untouchability, Temple entry of Dalits,* the internal politics of the *Congress Party,* and future of *Constitutionalism* in independent India.

Gandhi and Sastri referred to each other in those letter as "***brother***". All those letters between the two, fortunately, have been preserved in the Government of India archives and the **Gokhale Institute of Public Affairs** today as **"Gandhi-Sastri Letters".**

It is from the correspondence in those letters that I was able to cherry-pick three very interesting, *nay,* astounding ones that vividly showed how affectionately the two *"brothers" -in-arms,* although they differed fundamentally in their respective philosophical outlook in life and politics, could never snap mutual ties and bonding, never tear themselves away from nor fall out with each other.

A. In one correspondence, Gandhi endearingly conveyed to Sastri sentiments that showed how he had come to trust, in fact, the latter's instincts and political judgment more than he trusted that of even Gandhi's own son, *Manilal Gandhi.*

B. In another hilarious private correspondence, Sastri suggests corrections to Gandhi's inaugural published epistle in the "*Harijan,*" giving him superb grammar lessons on how sentence syntax in the English language must be structured. Gandhi accepts them all with all good-humoured humility and gratitude!

C. And in the third correspondence that I was able to pick, Sastri took the liberty to show Gandhi the mirror to his face, hinting in classic tongue-in-cheek manner at the latter's occasional saintly humbug… even nuisance… that did not really serve his own interests. Sastri then sternly advised him -- as one affectionate brother would another -- to stop being a "*dictator,*" for the sake of the good future of not only the *Indian National Congress* but also free India!

**** **** ****

Chapter 6
When Sastri corrected Gandhi's English sentence-syntax

Many of the scores of letters to Mahatma Gandhi that Srinivasa Sastri wrote were from his home in Mylapore, Madras (now Chennai). The house was named "***Swaagatham***" (*welcome*).

I have visited that house several times in the 1980s when *Karthik* (Sastri's great grandson), my friend and fellow Chartered Accountant, used to invite me there late afternoons for an hour or two, just to exchange and compare notes on how each was preparing for upcoming then final Chartered Accountancy examinations. So feverishly tense used to be our exam-preparations that simply to relieve ourselves of the pent-up nervous tension, we often used to play shuttle-badminton in the large front-yard of Sastri's home. After we had both sweated it out in a strenuous workout in a game or two, we'd relax and chat a bit, seated on old-style wicker-chairs kept out in the porch. Kathik later told me that when Gandhiji had visited Sastri at home for the very first time, he in fact had been seated at the exact spot in the porch where we were both then seated! Immediately I felt goosebumps on my skin in just imagining that where I had once sat on that porch in "*Swaagatham*" was where the Mahatma once had sat!

Karthik's mother, Srinivasa Sastri's granddaughter, Smt. Padmini Gopalan, a very kindly and gracious lady (she's now in her 90s and, bless her, still lives happily with son, Karthik), I remember used to serve us cool lemon juice or hot coffee to lift our spirits up and drive our examination blues away.

Sastri's "*swaagatham*" house was situated on *V.M. Street* (Venkatachala Mudali Street) that today veers off from *Dr Radhakrishna Salai to Luz, Mylapore* via the *Madras Sanskrit College* and *Thiruvalluvar Statue.* The house I remember was a very spacious, sprawling and stately bungalow adjacent to the *Children's Club.* It was a two-storied building with large frontage, airy rooms with vaulting high-roof, long cool verandas and broad balconies. Whenever I visited that house, in my mind, I couldn't help imagining the Rt. Hon'ble Srinivasa Sastri himself striding about in spirit around the very spot I happened to be standing upon.... It was a very humbling feeling indeed.

**** ****

One of the very first things that Sastri intended to do on his return to India from South Africa was to write from his home in "*Swaagatham*" a full-fledged report of his mission solely for the eyes of Mahatma Gandhi. He was aware that during his assignment in South Africa, many people from there as from within India itself too, had been feeding Gandhi in drips and dribbles with all sorts of information on Sastri's activities. Such informal and informant channels of communication were giving Gandhi positive feedback, generally, while a few others were funnelling also negative, specious stuff about him.

Gandhi's son **Manilal Gandhi** was one such person.

Manilal who lived in Durban South Africa was the Editor of a newspaper called "*The Indian Opinion*". It had, in fact, been founded earlier by Mahatma Gandhi himself. The newspaper was advocating for the rights of the Indian community and hence was also covering and publicising Sastri's activities as India's *Agent-General* there.

Initially, Manilal was extremely unhappy with Sastri's public speeches and stated positions on how he intended to serve the Indian community's cause in South Africa. He too, like many of Sastri's detractors, felt that Sastri was bending over backwards to ingratiate himself with the British Ruling dispensation in South Africa, trying to placate and appease them. In his letters to his father, Manilal minced no words about what he felt about Sastri's speeches and work.

Gandhi read his son Maniklal's letters and reports, however, with more than a pinch of salt. The Mahatma had greater faith in his friend Sastri than he had in his own son's instincts and political judgement. And he made no secret of his feelings directly to Sastri in a very candid and very affectionately worded letter.

My dear brother,

I am watching what is happening but consider it wise not to say anything. But I shall not hesitate to intervene when necessary.

What I find disturbing is a para in ***Manilal's*** *letter which I translate below:*

"I am not quite satisfied with his speeches. He crosses the limits in praising the Empire and the benefits conferred by it in India. He thinks it necessary thus to please the Europeans. He seems to believe that thus only shall we secure something. The effect of these speeches cannot be good in India. He (the magazine publisher) has therefore asked me not to print them in " Indian Opinion."

He has not the faculty of discrimination to see that we are like blood brothers even though we do not hold the same views about the Empire. I have not said to him much about this letter of his beyond warning him against coming to hasty judgements and telling him that you do honestly believe the Empire activity to be on the whole beneficial.

But you will of course not hesitate to summon him before you and ***speak to him if necessary as you would to your own son****... For he is a good boy and brave boy...*

Sastri had been keen to brief Gandhi through a comprehensive report of his mission in South Africa to disabuse him of any negative impressions that the Mahatma might have gathered from the malicious drip-by-drip feedback fed to him by some quarters that included even Manilal, the

Mahatma's son. Sastri felt that if Gandhi was convinced about the success of his South African mission, he needed to worry little about what others in the INC or elsewhere thought about him.

However, to Sastri's chagrin, he could not send in such a report since Gandhi at that time was serving a sentence in jail in *Yerawada.*

" (I felt) the first thing to do on return to the shores of India was to go to Mahatma Gandhi and make a report to him of our doings. To no one could a prior report be made. If he approved of our work, that was enough-- this was the feeling not merely of myself, who may be considered to have a weakness for Mahatma Gandhi, but of all with whom I was associated (as colleagues). And if I may for the first time publish a secret, it was also the feeling of the members of the Government of India. How sad I must feel now, you can imagine, when it is not possible for me to make similar report to the one man in all India who has a right to form a judgement of South African affairs and lead public sentiment in the country!"

Gandhi of course, as his later correspondence below reveals -- and before Sastri's return to India and the submission of his intended report – openly acknowledged that the trust he had had placed in Sastri to do the job in South Africa stood completely vindicated. And that he had also been right not to place too much trust in his son Maniklal's assessment of Sastri's work.

SABARMATI: 26th February 1928

My dear Brother,

I have been duly receiving the duplicates of your demi-official notes for Sir Muhammad Habibullah. Manilal and others keep me informed of your movements. Already urgent letters are being received to implore you not to leave South Africa at the end of your year. They say you are already counting your months. And they are trembling in their shoes, and more than they, am I trembling, and perhaps my trembling is weightier because of the absence of shoes. For, I really feel that except for grave reasons of health it would be a national tragedy for you to leave South Africa at the present moment. And I am sorry to have to say-- but it is true -- that no one else can successfully replace you at the present moment. The familiarity that your stay in South

Africa might have produced has certainly not bred contempt; on the contrary, it has gained greater respect for you from those whose respect counts for the work.

And just as you have gained influence amongst the Europeans, you have gained staunch adherents amongst our own countrymen. You may not desert them. Do please therefore let me have a reassuring letter. Of course, I don't know what the Government may want you to do.

With love, Yours sincerely

M. K. GANDHI

P.S: *If you were here, you would not appreciate our polities just now.*

**** ****

Mahatma Gandhi, amongst the many versatile qualities that he possessed, was also a prolific writer and correspondent. His himself founded a magazine called "*Harijan*". Through countrywide circulation of this magazine, Gandhi intended to keep up a continuous line of mass communication with vast followers and countrymen across India.

Anyone during that period of the Freedom Struggle who wished to know Gandhi's thinking, ideas or his mind on any matter of national importance -- be it political, economic, social, religious or spiritual -- would have had to subscribe to and read regularly the Mahatma's epistles published in the *Harijan.*

After the inaugural issue of *Harijan* was printed and went into circulation, Gandhi sent a copy of it to Srinivasa Sastri to elicit his editorial opinion on it and especially on the lead article the Mahatma had authored. The ensuing correspondence between Sastri and Gandhi was meant to be private but then Gandhi found it to be not only hilarious but also so very educative that he had had Sastri's letter subsequently published for public consumption!

After reading Gandhi's article in the *Harijan,* Sastri picked up and pointed out to him half a dozen faults in grammar, syntax and style in the content. Sastri proved his school-headmaster background to a tee! Gandhi accepted Sastri's masterly lessons on the finer aspects of English grammar and composition with all the good grace, humour, humility and the gratitude of a middle-school boy in class!

"I wrote to the Rt. Hon. Srinivasa Sastri for a message to the ' ***Harijan****'. And I received a characteristic reply marked 'private'. The letter seemed to me to be too good to be suppressed. I, therefore, wired for permission to publish it. The reply wire was as characteristic as the letter.*

"Firstly, inappropriate to 'Harijan', secondly offensive to partisans, ill requital for your steadfast affection.

However, if perchance useful, please publish."

And here is the letter below.

Private

MYLAPORE: ***13th February 1933***

Dear Brother**,**

Thanks for your affectionate letter, in which you ask for a message to your new baby.

I am going to charge towards you. It is necessary in your interest, no matter what effort it costs me.

You live in a difficult world. Waking or dreaming, you are racked by thoughts of sin and penance, confessions and truth-quests, *satyagraha* and moral self-flagellation. Those having sent home my dart of criticism, I folded my hands and prayed. "*Enlighten me, for my soul is cast in doubt and you know all.*"

"I have written objecting to (your) too frequent references to the Inner Voice" that talk to you or correspond with you continually pose doubts and serious problems, only deepening the grimness and suffocation around you. Few bring lightness of talk, familiar expletives, innocent jokes, revealing banter. *You badly need a privileged jester in your establishment.*

Have you read a story called *Ardath by Ouida*? The hero there has a critic whose business is to expose his errors and bring to light the flaws in his character. Being a professional faultfinder, he overdoes his part in the end and defeats his first object. I shall vary my function from time to time and disappear from the scene every now and then. But I will endeavour to awaken parts of your mind long gone to sleep and to supply elements of nourishment which it has long been without. Of course, you can stop the medicine if it disagrees and you cannot stand it! That would be a sign to me that the disease had gone too far.

You are an extraordinarily correct writer of English. The ordinary reader will not detect any slips on your part. They are not only rare but of a subtle nature. The eye of a schoolmaster, made acute by dwelling on trivialities of grammar, can alone see them. Here are some, all from the first number of the '*Harijan*' and from the parts bearing your name.

Page 3. "*If it is a bye-product of the caste system, it is only in the same sense that an ugly growth is of a body.*" ('*That*' is fast undergoing a change in English, but this use is far in excess of present usage. Better say' *in which an ugly growth is a bye-product of a body.*')

Also read the whole passage again. Don't you say in effect '*If the caste system is a bye-product of the caste system?*'

Page 3. "*The outcaste-ness, in the sense we understand it, has therefore to be destroyed altogether.*" (A slip similar to the above. Between '*sense*' and '*we*', insert '*in which*'.)

Page 4. "*Caste Hindus have to open their temples to Harijans, precisely on the same terms as the other Hindus.*" (Say ' *the same terms as* ' to ' *the other Hindus*'. Else, it would mean that the other Hindus opened their temples on certain terms to Harijans.)

Page 7. "*Beyond this I may not go, for the reason I have already stated and which the reader should respect.*" (Insert 'which' *after* '*reason*'. The conjunction '*and*' must not be made to connect a suppressed '*which*' and an expressed '*which.*')

Page 8. "*Untouchability has a great deal to answer for the insanitation of our streets and our latrines.*" ('Idiomatically, '*for*' is part of the verb ' *answer*' and cannot govern '*the insanitation*'. We must insert '*in*' after '*for*', though the sentence becomes inelegant. I would recast it: ' *Untouchability is answerable for a great deal of the insanitation &c.*').

Page 8. "*Therefore, a person who is to attend to scavenging, whether it is a paid Bhangi or an unpaid mother, they are unclean until they have washed themselves clean of their unclean work.*"

(The looseness is, perhaps, the result of rapid dictation unchecked by subsequent reading. '*A person*' is left hanging in the air. The plurals '*they*', '*themselves*' and '*their*' are justified by the common gender required.

Still, the discord of number is apparent to the point of harshness and may be avoided. Read ' *A person is unclean until washed clean of the unclean work.*')

Let me add a criticism of substance.

On **page 7** you answer a question under the heading "*Seeking or Giving?*" The paragraph has gained brevity at the expense of clearness. The difference between giving cooperation and seeking it requires more elucidation. Likewise, the analogy of love leading to feeding in one case and starving in another. But you are obscure and even baffling when you say that your policy of non-cooperation with Government allows of your seeking its cooperation whenever your purpose is, in your opinion, *"very sacred and altogether good*". Most sensible people follow this rule in ordinary life: *not seeking co-operation when they don't care* and *seeking it when they care.* They don't proclaim it as a policy or give it a grand name.

Ever yours affectionately

V. S. SRINIVASAN

**** ****

Gandhi went on to add another footnote-comment after reproducing in full Sastri's *Letter* verbatim in the next issue of *Harijan*:

I wanted to share this letter with the public, because such a letter would help any publicist and his cause and that in an unexpected manner, more so when written without any thought of publication.

Let the student note in passing Sastri's love for the language he has mastered as few men have done. He is a purist in everything. We badly need purists in our country. I want only purists as fellow workers in this glorious campaign of abolition of untouchability.

As to the purity of the language of ' Harijan', whatever faults are found notwithstanding Sastri's warning will be shared with me by Sastri, the

Editor, and by Mahadev Desai, who shares with the schoolmaster the weakness for writing correctly in the language which for the moment he is using.

I must leave the reader to find out for himself or herself the many other beauties of Sastri's letter. If he will do so, he must read the letter three or four times and look up all the references in the first issue of 'Harijan'.

M. K. GANDHI

**** ****

Today, those of us who admire Gandhi and Sastri ... and still love the beauties of the English language... would do well indeed, as Gandhi had urged, to *"read the letter three or four times and look up all the references in the first issue of 'Harijan."*

**** **** ****

Chapter 7
A brave character-profiling of the Mahatma

In their philosophical approach regarding how the struggle for India's Freedom from British Colonial Rule must be conducted, Srinivasa Sastri and Mahatma Gandhi were indeed poles apart.

Gandhi looked upon himself as a *saint-politician.* Sastri looked upon himself as *scholar-statesman.* The contrast between the two men stood out starkly at times whenever Gandhi chose to *weaponize his spiritualism* and use it as a political tactical attack against the British establishment. Sastri, on the other hand, many a time *weaponized his liberal value-system* to shame British conscience and their sense of political fair play.

Gandhi's most preferred weapon thus was **militant Satyagraha** while Sastri's standard weapon was **militant constitutionalism**, both of which although fundamentally rooted in *Ahimsa*, India's civilisational principle of **Non-Violence**, nonetheless and not too rarely, led to the two friends being at odds with each other.

An incident in 1933 happened which reveals the sharply contrasting philosophical outlook and political operating-styles of Sastri and Gandhi as they had always existed and simmered beneath their otherwise brotherly relationship.

**** ****

Gandhi wrote the below letter to Sastri in Mylapore:

2nd May 1933

My dear Brother

Dare I ask for your blessings for the coming Yajna? It is now nearing 2 a.m. I have left my bed among other things to write this begging letter. If the fast does not meet with your approval, I know you are too true a brother to grant my request merely to please me. With love, Yours

M. K. GANDHI

The "*yajna*" (observance of a sacrificial rite) that Gandhi was referring to in the letter was an intended twenty-one day fast that the Mahatma had resolved to voluntarily undertake from the **8th to 29th May 1933** in the Yerawada Prison. What was the reason for such a fast?

Gandhiji claimed it was part of his *"Harijan work"* i.e. his passionate campaign championing the cause of Harijan emancipation from caste oppression, abolition of *Untouchability* and social advancement of the Harijan population in India. However, Gandhi's expression "*purification of self and my associates...*" was intriguing since there was a larger background story behind it. But before that story can be recounted here, first it is to Sastri's reply to Gandhi's letter that must be reproduced and read carefully so that the context can be understood.

This is Sastri's letter below. In it we see him clearly tell the Mahatma right to his face that the idea of fasting does not fit in at all with Sastri's own philosophical convictions. In a very gentle, subtle and characteristically inoffensive manner, Sastri also expresses his dismay at what we may today perhaps recognize to be mystic mumbo-jumbo with which the Mahatma oftentimes disguised his pious self-flagellation:

Private

MYLAPORE: *7th May 1933*

Dearest Brother,

After much thought and destruction of several drafts, I have decided that the best reply to your 'begging' and most touching letter of the 2nd instant is the enclosed extract (i.e. in which Gandhi had stated "'It is particularly prayer for the purification of self and my associates. I want more workers of unassailable purity'). I trust it will sustain you ever so little in the ordeal which will have begun when it reaches Yeravada.

It would have been useless and, as you said in your first statement, embarrassing for me to try to dissuade. What remains for your friends and associates is to wish that you may come out of the ordeal not merely unscathed but armed afresh with the strength of 'tapas' for the struggle that seems without end.

I will not pretend for a moment that I approve of your fast. To one like me, born in Hinduism and bred up in it for long years, the arguments pro and con are thoroughly familiar. From sacred texts one might confute most of the reasoning in your statements. But beyond texts and mere authority is reason and humanity, on which you habitually fall back. Even in that ultimate court I fear we shall not be found on the same side.

Our values are different fundamentally. The difference is radical; no sophistry can abolish it.

In spite of what you have said in the last revelation of your heart, I believe that too much self-communion and internal debate have undermined your judgement. The state of ecstasy when values are reversed, when day becomes night and night day, when pleasure becomes pain and pain pleasure, is rare even in the experience of mystics. The attempt to make it habitual and to adopt the language appropriate to that state as the language of everyday speech is, if I may use the expression, to walk on moral stilts. On occasions you appear to me, in strange contrast to your realism, to impose that mode of movement on the common men and women around you.

The atmosphere in such circumstances is apt to be thick with disappointment and grievous failure. And if the only correction possible were self-correction, the master must needs find himself doomed to the cell of penitence, which is next door to suicide. You have enough philosophy to understand that to claim divine sanction for a course of conduct is to withdraw it from the field of discussion and deprive it of direct validity to other minds. Whenever I come across the claim in your writing, I cannot help quoting to myself the famous line of Kalidasa:

"विचार्येषुः प्रतिभासि मे त्वम्।"

You appear to me to be confounded by anxious thought.

I cannot tell you how much I deplore the publication of the story of ***Nila Nagini Devi.*** *If it were merely a confession, I might understand it, though it would still repel me as the exposure of one's sores. But why should you rub it in? The moral proclaims itself. Here again it is a deep-going disparity of taste. I am still in the grip of the world's idea of decorum. You have gone beyond and would repudiate low standards. With great effort I remind myself that hagiology is full of such records, and I must somehow get reconciled.*

I did not mean to write at length, but the stuff inside has forced itself on your attention. Don't mind it. Treat the letter as if it were nothing but the expression of my unchanged love and of my fervent wish that you should live long and serve the great causes you cherish. For, contrary to your teaching, I hold that you are more potent than your memory can be.

With affectionate thoughts, Yours always

V. S. SRINIVASAN

**** ****

Sastri minced no words in saying to Gandhi point-blank that *"Our values are different fundamentally. The difference is radical; no sophistry can abolish it"*.

Sastri often found it tiresome to hear his friend Gandhi go on and on often moralising on even matters that were political and worldly and nothing to do with the spiritual. He even openly expressed his impatience with the Mahatma's frequent invocation of his so-called "***inner voice***"... Gandhi himself was quite aware of Sastri's impatience and wrote a tad apologetically in another letter of his (1932):

"I do wish I never spoke of God or the Inner Voice or Conscience. But, like "Ramnaam", however much it may be abused, it has got to be repeated when it is relevant and almost becomes imperative. Truth will receive a deep cut if, for fear of being misunderstood or even being called a fraud, I did not say boldly what I felt to be true."

The other interesting line in Sastri's letter is his reference to **"Nila Nagini Devi."** He expresses mortification in no uncertain terms at Gandhi having written about it publicly which he describes as *"a deep-going disparity of taste"* ... *"that repels me as the exposure of one's sores."*

*** ***

Who was "*Nila Nagini Devi*"? *What was she to Mahatma Gandhi? Why did Gandhi bring her name up in the context of his 21-day fast, championing at Yerawada the Harijan cause? What did she have to do with Gandhi's "Harijan work?"*

Ms. Nilla Cram Cook was an attractive American lady who had come to India in search of spiritual solace and self-discovery. Thanks to some friends in Ahmedabad, she had ended up as a volunteer *sevak* at the ***Ashram*** and an ardent disciple of Mahatma Gandhi himself with whom she began profusely corresponding on a host of Indian social issues such as Harijan upliftment and abolition of *Untouchability*, a cause that was very close to Gandhi's heart. Ms. Cook began calling herself **Nila Nagini Devi** in all her correspondence with Gandhi.

To fully understand why in his letter to Sastri, Gandhi had referred to his 21-day proposed fasting as a "*yajna*" as a "***prayer for the purification of self and my associates***", it becomes necessary to know a little background about *Nila Nagini Devi.* In an article (https://www.theindiaforum.in/book-reviews/gandhis-american-disciple), *Gangeya Mukherjee* explains to us what this American lady-disciple was to Gandhi.

QUOTE: "The account of Ms. Cook's life in India makes for painful reading. Cook, or *Nila Nagini Devi* as she was also known, swirled in the currents of her mercurial temperament, her lack of inhibitions and striking beauty, drawing admirers to her. They were willing to provide her with logistical support for indulging her numerous itinerant whims, including introducing her to Indian royalty. Individuals as varied as ministers of Indian princes, venerable pedants, staid journalists such as Durga Das, and countless youths from all sorts of backgrounds were participants in her enterprises.

"Born to a broken marriage between bohemian American parents, raised for some years in Greece, married and divorced at a very young age, and generally disillusioned with life in the West, the talented and versatile Cook arrived in Kashmir in 1931 with her young child. Bereft quite soon of her inheritance, scarred by exploitative physical relationships, and with spiritual bliss still elusive, she found solace in Harijan service, having been introduced to it by Thakkar, the secretary of the **Harijan Sevak Sangh**. Her contact with Gandhi and his *anti-untouchability* campaign of 1932 soon followed.

"Beginning in November 1932, within the space of hardly a year, Cook wrote what can only be described as a flurry of letters to Gandhi, receiving usually prompt, though not always the expected, responses from him. Her letters, graduating from the initial address of *"Revered Mahatma-ji"* and signed as *"ever yours in service and devotion, Nila Nagini"* to the final phase with *"Beloved Bapu"* and *"With all our love, Nila,"* contain her thoughts and plans for Harijan service, and many other things.

"They (the letters) express her weakness before a desire that blurs both social norms and ethical principles; they complain about the hardships of slum housing or the defects of the *Satyagraha Ashram*; and they agonise about her physical ailments and those of her son and even speak of her menstrual problems. The letters plead for guidance and nearness. As the volume reveals, Gandhi's responses—even when he seems on the verge of giving up on her for her immorality and weakness before desire—never waver in their caring tone. He advises her on her diet and spiritual upliftment, on a pregnancy after an indiscreet encounter with a youth volunteer in Harijan service and is solicitous about the welfare of her son. Gandhi remains, to all intents and purposes, a combination of a father and a mother to her.

"After a troubled stint in the Harijan cause and increasing restlessness in *Satyagraha Ashram*, Cook left Ahmedabad in October 1933, without informing Gandhi, never to return. Only a few letters were exchanged between them after this."

"Gandhi's relationship with Cook illustrates the natural affinity that women usually felt towards him, and his own conception of his generally filial approach towards participants of his movements, particularly the inmates of his ashrams."

"It also illustrates his rare understanding of the enchantment of regarding service to Harijans as an exotic experience other than an expiatory one, which made it necessary for one to be very vigilant against exploiting the vulnerabilities of the deprived and disinherited. Most of all, it illustrates the sacrality that Gandhi perceived in the Harijan cause, any other word being inadequate to describe its place in his moral universe."

"Cook's brief but disappointing relationship with Rudramani, a Harijan youth (in the *Ashram*), jolted Gandhi. Although in this case he was critical of Rudramani's conduct, on the general plane, it rudely brought home to him the possibility of helpless men and women being treated as emotional and physical prey by volunteers turned predators, all in the guise of service. He was very aware that in informal interactions between young and healthy men and women, erotic desire could be at the root of attraction though it could be camouflaged as a spiritual yearning for a higher cause." **UNQUOTE**

So, the fast that Gandhi told Sastri he was going to undertake was thus "*prayer for the purification of self and my associates*" and a way to atone for a sexual scandal that had happened at *Satyagraha Ashram* in which a Harijan was both victim and perpetrator. And that was the real cause of such intense mystic agony for Gandhi's troubled *"inner voice,"* and which had thus compelled him to perform a self-imposed "*yajna!*" And all this according to Gandhi was part of his "*Harijan work!*"

Sastri himself confessed that he had found it all very hard to get reconciled to and so he wrote candidly to Gandhi:

"... if the only correction possible were self-correction, the master must needs find himself doomed to the cell of penitence, which is next door to suicide. You have enough philosophy to understand that to claim divine sanction for a course of conduct is to withdraw it from the field of discussion and deprive it of direct validity to other minds".... I believe that too much self-communion and internal debate have undermined your judgement. The state of ecstasy when values are reversed, when day becomes night and night day, when pleasure becomes pain and pain pleasure, is rare even in the experience of mystics. The attempt to make it habitual and to adopt the language appropriate to that state as the language of everyday speech is, if I may use the expression, to walk on moral stilts. On occasions you appear to me, in strange contrast to your realism, to impose that mode of movement on the common men and women around you."

**** ****

What a brave but so very accurate character-profiling of the great man whom the whole of India hero-worshipped as a ***Mahatma***!

**** **** ****

Chapter 8
Stop being a dictator, step away from Congress Party

Srinivasa Sastry respected Mahatma Gandhi for his deeply spiritual aspirations. But Gandhi's *spiritual militancy*, such as his agitational methods of *Satyagraha* employed against the British, received only his grudging admiration. And even such admiration was often conveyed to the Mahatma only with a large dose of brotherly and typically "*inoffensive*" admonition.

Sastri as a friend advised Gandhi that his great ***"experiments with Truth"*** that consisted of mixing political work with spiritual "*saadhana*" -- such as fasting, self-abnegation and self-flagellation practises -- was not a healthy idea. It was, in fact, Sastri said, Gandhi's "*disease of grimness*". He told Gandhi that it was that *disease* that caused all his mental disturbances and depressive states. It turned his political engagement often into an obsession with personal angst, agony and self-doubt leading eventually to the Mahatma's not infrequent bouts of melancholy.

In one of his most affectionate letters to Gandhi, Sastri wrote asking the Mahatma to stop meditating on his navel, as it were to cheer up instead and to stop brooding over his spiritual failings, and to surround himself with less grim and more jovial friends and colleagues.

"You live in a difficult world. Waking or dreaming, you are racked by thoughts of sin and penance, confessions and truth-quests, satyagraha and moral self-flagellation. Those having sent home my dart of criticism, I folded my hands and prayed. "Enlighten me, for my soul is cast in doubt and you know all."

The atmosphere in such circumstances is apt to be thick with disappointment and grievous failure. And if the only correction possible were self-correction, the master must needs find himself doomed to the cell of penitence, which is next door to suicide.... You appear to me to be confounded by anxious thought.

"I have written objecting to (your) too frequent references to the "Inner Voice" that talk to you or correspond with you, continually pose doubts and serious problems, only deepening the grimness and suffocation around you. Few bring lightness of talk, familiar expletives, innocent jokes, revealing banter. ***You badly need a privileged jester in your establishment."***

**** ****

In response to Sastri's suggestion to cheer up and fill his surroundings with "*lightness of talk, familiar expletives, innocent jokes, banter ...*", Gandhi replied chirping to his friend in Mylapore, telling him that he very much appreciated especially the suggestion to appoint a "*jester within the establishment*" whose job would be to keep his spirits up from falling into the pit of melancholy.

"Let them learn that closest friendships can subsist between persons of contrary temperaments. As the public know, Sastri and I have opposite views on many important questions. Our mutual regard and affection have never suffered on

that account. There is no reason whatsoever why the same rule cannot be extended to parties and groups representing opposite schools of opinion (in our politics) .... *Would that the affection subsisting between Sastri and me prove so deep and extensive as to reach and affect the whole society!*

"*But enough of this. I almost hear Sastri's spirit whispering to me: 'You are misusing the medicine I prescribed to wean you from your disease of grimness and the like'. Therefore, let me hasten to tell him and the public that I have in my little camp of four a specially privileged jester in* ***Sardar Vallabhbhai Patel.*** *He succeeds in bending me almost double every day with laughter over his unexpected sallies. Gloom hides her fiendish face in his presence. No disappointment, however great, can make him gloomy for long. And he will not let me be serious for two consecutive minutes He will not spare even my 'saintliness'! It may deceive simple people but never the Sardar ... (he) tear(s) down the mask and compel(s) me to see myself as ... (perhaps Sastri might) delight to see me.... The thing that Sastri wants in our little family is there, cent per cent. Next time he enters the Assembly or some such place, he must vote special thanks to the Government for putting Vallabhbhai with me or me with him.*

But this consoling information does not in any way release Sastri from his self-imposed obligation. For the Sardar will not do what Sastri can be trusted to do mostly. Unlike him, the Sardar has the wretched habit in the end of saying 'ditto' to all I say. And that is bad for anybody.

**** ****

The admonitory tone of Sastri's letters to his friend Gandhi was reserved not only for matters personal but also included political affairs and especially, on occasions, when Sastri felt Gandhi was carrying *Satyagraha* to extremes.

In **August 1933**, while in prison, Gandhi threatened the British authorities with what came to be called the ***'Harijan facilities fast"***.

On 1st August, the Mahatma and his chosen band of individual resisters had been arrested at Sabarmati. Gandhiji was released on 4th August, and immediately after served with an order restricting his movements. On disobeying the order, he was re-arrested. Release and re-arrest happened also to his followers.

Soon after his arrest, Gandhiji wrote to the Government seeking permission for the use in prison of what he called the freedom to use "*facilities for Harijan work*" which he had enjoyed as prisoner in 1932. It meant that even while from prison, Gandhi be allowed to engage in political activity (such as *writing, publishing, broadcasting, giving interviews, propagandizing* etc.) outside so long as it was related to Harijan causes and Harijan welfare. On the 14th instant, after Gandhi had sent four reminders and announced his intention to fast, the Government reluctantly gave him certain *facilities* but imposed certain conditions. He was to give no interviews for publication in the press.

Gandhiji considered the facilities granted thus to him as "*far short of the original orders of the Government of India and of my requirements.*" It was clear, he said, that the Government gave the facilities grudgingly. They had, moreover, passed an unfair criticism that whenever the Mahatma was free, he only devoted more time, in fact, to political work than to Harijan work. So, Gandhiji went immediately on a fast on the 16th of August. The British however released him on the 23rd instant.

Sastri was not aware of the entire correspondence that had been earlier exchanged between Gandhi and the British authorities. But from whatever he learned about the *Satyagraha* staged inside the prison, he made it clear that he felt it arose more from either Gandhi's wonted petulance or from a surge of intemperate indignation that the Mahatma felt against the British and far less from any overriding sense of sympathy for the Harijan cause.

Sastri's frank view was expressed in a letter to Gandhi that he wrote. This letter has reference to what is called the *"Harijan Facilities Fast"* which resulted in Gandhiji's release on the seventh day and transfer to *Parna Kuti* where he broke the fast. Sastri had evidently no access to the long correspondence that had taken place earlier between Government and Gandhiji. So, all that he however insisted in his letter was that the privileges Gandhi had enjoyed as prisoner during the year 1932, could not be demanded in 1933 or every time the British saw cause to place him under arrest. That to Sastri was untenable.

Expressing rare disappointment and exasperation which he felt over Gandhi ji's near-anarchist methods of agitation, Sastri then went on in the letter to urge the Mahatma to even (a) **give up *Civil Disobedience,*** (b) **to rein in his own dictatorial tendencies as the leader of the *Indian National Congress,*** (c) **to quit the Party and** (d) **to let its**

younger leaders start shouldering the burden of carrying on the freedom struggle!

Sastri also advised Gandhi to instead focus all his energies and attention on building the **blueprint of a modern Constitutional architecture** for the independent nation that India was bound to emerge as, sooner or later, and in any case, not too far in the future, given the imminent collapse of Imperial Britain.

COIMBATORE: 27th August 1933

Dearest Brother,

Government might well have given you the old facilities. A curse has disabled them from generous or timely action. But they haven't conferred a right on you or made you a promise. What they conceded to you at one time and in one set of conditions they are not bound to concede to you at another time and in another set of conditions The order made (earlier) after the Poona Pact, from which you quote, does not amount to an irrevocable or unconditional promise. You indulge in special pleading of a bad type when you charge them with a breach of promise. The addition of the words 'made to a prisoner in their custody' (made by you) loses the point it might have had otherwise.

It might be said by an observer who wasn't prejudiced against Government that, while Harijan uplift was dear to you, putting blame on Government was dearer. It has been said in my hearing by well-disposed persons that you would love nothing so much as to die in gaol and leave Government burdened with the responsibility.

Behind and beyond your present tussle with Government lies the future of the country. How can Congress best secure that future? Your answer is clear. But another answer is taking shape in people's minds. ***It is that civil disobedience, both mass and individual, must be given up.***

A new policy, aiming at constructive national good in legislation, finance and administration all round, has long been overdue and must be tried over and above what is now called the ***constructive programme of Congress****. I believe this feeling is common outside Congress and is gaining ground inside Congress. How can this orientation be brought about?*

It is so different from your present polices, in look so opposed to it, that one doubts whether you can undertake it. Perhaps your whole preparation and equipment lie in a different direction. It is no disparagement to anyone that he is not fitted to lead the nation in all contingencies and in all directions. Unfortunately, no man, however big, can be always trusted to know his limitations and make room when the cause to which he is devoted requires it. His very greatness stands in the way of change. And as I have told you more than once, you have outtopped all other leaders so long and so decisively that there is no man in sight to take your place at once.

What a blessing it would he if you could be transformed and re-made, as it were, for the fresh era. But you are too good, too true to yourself to pretend you are the same teacher when the creed is no longer yours and the ritual is something you have never conducted.

In this sore strait, the country looks to you to play a greater part than you have ever played. (Pardon me: what I mean is the greater part of the country as I figure out the parties). Save your individual conscience, pursue civil disobedience, seek the goal and embarrass Government as you like; but leave Congress free to evolve a new programme. It simply cannot do so, while it has to give authority and countenance to individual disobedience.

You remember I begged you to adopt this course when I was last with you at Parna Kuti. You told me you put it to the working committee, but they would have none of it. Naturally and in a way properly too. The committee couldn't face the odium of abandoning you. I don't wonder the thought was abhorrent to them. The moment is come-- in my opinion it came long ago--for you to say, 'I set Congress free to try other methods. I have plenty of God's work to do, for the nation's welfare, with Harijans'.

There, then, I've told you the truth as it seems to me.

May one hope that you will see the problem from a new angle. I know one thing. There is no self-effacement to which you are not equal. The only thing is it must seem to you to be called for.

All that a friend and brother can do is to give an indication.

Yours affectionately

V. S. SRINIVASAN

**** ****

To Srinivasa Sastri's very blunt but equally sincere and friendly message to him, Gandhi replied defensively as follows in a slightly hurt, acerbic yet unoffended tone:

30th August 1933: Parna Kuti

Dear Brother

I treasure your letter.

I do not mind anything you have said. On the contrary I appreciate all you have said. Having said this, I must say that I utterly dissent from your interpretation of Government orders. If you saw all the correspondence, perhaps you will revise your judgement. I am not given to special pleading consciously. You may not have noticed that the Government have themselves dropped the idea of 'another set of conditions.' On the contrary, they said that they made a mistake in making what you call 'concession in the first instance', and the mistake made was not one on merits but had reference to their own convenience.

However, I shall not strive with you in connection with your pronouncement upon my statement, but if you will care to study the whole question, I would gladly send you the whole of the correspondence. I hope that you yourself do not consider me to be capable of desiring to blame the government for the sake of doing so or that that performance would be dearer to me than Harijan uplift. I consider myself capable of a just discrimination and therefore of knowing when the Government is in the right.

But this is all beside the point. I have taken so much space with what is now immaterial, in order to tell you that I do not plead guilty to the charge you have made against me.

Now for the central point of your letter. I quite agree with you that I am wholly **unfit for the constitution building** *at the present stage. In my opinion that time is not yet. It will come only when the nation has developed a sanction for itself. I would therefore gladly retire from the Congress and devote myself to the development of civil disobedience outside the Congress and to Harijan work. The difficulty is how to do it? Can I do it by seceding from the*

Congress? That was the question that troubled me at the time of the informal conference and that is the question that confronts me again. I am seeking light.

As soon as I have regained sufficient strength, I shall again sound the mind of Congressmen and if I can possibly retire from the Congress I shall gladly do so. ***My impression, however, is that the Congress mentality has not changed.*** *Whilst it is true that a large number of Congressmen have got tired, very few would care to subscribe to the* **white paper** *or work for securing certain improvements in it. They want a radical change. But I am in no hurry to come to any final decision. I can give you this assurance that nothing will deter me from taking any steps that might he in the best interests of the nation. There is no question even of self-effacement. Performance of duty I have held always to be a thing of beauty and a joy for ever. The awful fact, however, has often been to know where duty lies.*

You won't give me up but continue to guide me and you will not hesitate to come if you felt like coming.

I am not going to hesitate to ask you to come when I feel that I need your personal contact and a constant exchange of thoughts.

Love

M. K. GANDHI

**** ****

Sastri immediately replied to Gandhi's letter, providing more clarification on what he had intended to convey to the Mahatma:

COIMBATORE: 4th September 1933

Dear brother

I was touched by your reply. It was full and reasoned.

Neither of us forms an opinion in a hurry or drops it in a hurry. But there is a satisfaction in knowing the other side. In all circumstances, we shall carefully understand and make allowances for each other.

So let us dismiss the past.

I plead for Congress being freed from your rule. If you wait for its consent to the course, a very long delay is inevitable. Grant the freedom immediately.

Must you like the British Raj, put off the consummation till it becomes inevitable?

Certainly, Congress is not going to bother about improving on the ***white paper****. With the Tories in power and* ***our minorities clamouring for alms,*** *which is an impossible dream. Few progressive politicians in India indulge in it anymore.*

You write in your letter of forging a national sanction. Let one assume for a moment that yours is the only way of doing it, still must it be in point of time continuous absolutely without intermission or respite to the nation?

May it not be, in certain conditions, another way can be tried with advantage? The belief is widespread that such conditions are now in being. I will name two of these.

(1) The ascendancy of the Tories which looks likely to last long. (2) The danger to Indian Nationalism from the passing of the political power into the hands of minorities backed by and dependent on the British people.

If the ill effects of these conditions should be kept at a minimum, the national forces must combine effectively and must make themselves felt in all directions and all the time. 'Victory or Nothing' is a rousing cry on the battlefield. When the day is lost, it has no meaning.

Where legislatures exist, even such manacled legislatures as ours, much may be done, were it only to prevent evil by vigilant opposition. It is first rate to be the Government. If you can't be that the next best thing is to be a strong united opposition. Bacon said we must have our hands constantly in affairs, and he was a man of the world.

I know you have no faith in this method. But do not forget it takes all sorts to make a world. 'God fulfils Himself in many ways lest one good custom should corrupt the world.'

You seemed to think, when we last talked of this matter, that one wing of Congress might apply this method while another wing went on with individual Civil Disobedience.

I am clear the two methods are utterly incompatible.

Congress must choose one. Nor can the liberal and progressive schools be trusted to employ their methods on the necessary scale or with appreciable effect.

I am a liberal, but not so partisan as not to see the nation's good except through liberal spectacles. *It is my heart's wish that Congress and liberals and others similarly devoted to the cause of the future nation should merge and form one large party. But the idea is too good for the moment. We must be content to have these parties, with their several labels but cooperating for common purposes, as clearly defined as possible.*

If there is sense in this plan, pray give it a chance. Two conditions are necessary. Civil Disobedience must go. Dictatorship must go.

Yours lovingly

V. S. SRINIVASAN

**** ****

The reply that Gandhi dispatched back to Sastri revealed at once his mind on who his political successor was going to be! And that was an unambiguous hint conveyed to Sastri: that the time had, at last, come when "*the old order changed, yielding place to new*"!

PARNAKUTI: 9th September 1933

My dear Brother

I like your letter.

I want you to continue to strive with me and believe, as Gokhale used to believe of me, that whilst I often appeared to be uncompromising, I had a compromising and accommodating nature. I have always prized the certificate that he gave me and have endeavoured to live up to it.

If the freedom that you desire for the Congress was in my giving, I assure you that I would give it today, but it is not such a simple performance. When at Patna I surrendered all powers to the Swaraj party, Moti Lalji (Motilal Nehru) handsomely admitted that, though I was always ready to give, the party was only then (unready) to take them. The fact is that I do not want power. I look upon it as a privileged service. The moment I feel that I can get out of it to the benefit of the Congress, I will not fail.

However, you may depend upon me that I shall strain every nerve to adopt your advice. ***A great deal will depend upon Jawaharlal, whom I expect here on Saturday.***

Love

M. K. GANDHI

**** ****

That very last line in Gandhi's letter – *"A great deal will depend upon Jawaharlal, whom I expect here on Saturday"* -- was the biblical *"writing on the wall"* that he hoped Srinivasa Sastri would read, absorb and understand its full implications.

The Rt. Hon'ble Srinivasa Sastry's philosophy of constitutionalism and the liberal-humanist path he had always stoutly been advocating as the principal means to the end of **Swaraj** would not cut any ice in the new era that was dawning upon the political firmament of India under the **leadership of Jawaharlal Nehru**.

The last line, presaging as it did the rising spirit of **Indian Nationalism** also perhaps in a veiled way, signalled Srinivasa Sastri's imminent last bow and graceful exit.

**** **** ****

Chapter 9
The years in political wilderness

It would not be inaccurate to say that between 1933 and his death in 1946, Rt. Hon'ble V. S. Srinivasa Sastri was in relative political wilderness compared to his earlier prominence. By the mid-1930s, Sastri had distanced himself from the more militant and mass-based nationalist politics led by the *Indian National Congress* under Gandhi and Nehru, following his resignation from the Party over disagreements about the non-cooperation movement.

Sastri had serious qualms about *Civil Disobedience* and *Non-Cooperation* being used as weapons of political struggle albeit in Gandhian-style and in much-touted *Non-Violent* ways.

While not disagreeing that *Satyagraha* was indeed a very effective way of exerting tremendous moral pressure on the British Colonial powers, Sastri had the foresight, nevertheless, to realise that it was a potent and treacherous double-edged sword. After Independence was attained, Sastri feared, the new fledgling Nation might not be able to rein in the anarchic impulses that he discerned would always be lurking deep and latent at the very core of the whole philosophy of *Civil Disobedience.* Those impulses he felt would not be conducive to nation-building and, in fact, would turn out to be inimical to social reconstruction.

Civil Disobedience was politically expedient only in the short-term for Gandhi and Nehru who were keen to wrest freedom from the British. Sastri however was convinced that it would only instil in the Indian people, once freedom had been gained, a very unhealthy political culture and a deep-seated habit of wilful recalcitrance and non-cooperation that would never wear off from the psyche of the Indian people. It would only gather more strength and would engender and normalise chronic instability and acrimony in the relationship between the State and People.

In other words, Sastri had the statesman's farsightedness to anticipate how in the Independent Democratic Republic of India, Gandhi's legacy of Civil Disobedience would take very deep root in the national character and begin to constantly plague civil society with all sorts of mass-movements and social unrest, *dharna*, *hartal*, *andolan*, etc... all staged more for narrow parochial, group self-interests rather than large national causes. *Civil Disobedience* thus could easily become less and less *civil*; and in time, become ever increasingly more and more *disobedient*.

**** ****

During this later period in which he found himself in relative political wilderness, Sastri turned the focus of his energies to his other passions.

Sastri focused more on *constitutional liberalism* and worked through moderate political channels such as the *Indian Liberal Federation*. His leadership of the *Federation* and expertise as an orator and diplomat remained respected but his political influence and popular visibility diminished significantly in these years.

He engaged further in *diplomatic* and *educational* roles, notably serving as **Vice-Chancellor of Annamalai University** from 1935 to 1940. Since the British Government of India valued his expertise in foreign affairs, Sastri was even briefly offered an assignment to go to Malaya to study and submit a report on the status of Indian labourer-population working there as migrant workers in tea and rubber plantations.

Although Sastri participated in some important political events such as the **Round Table Conferences (1930-31)** and was part of delegations appealing for dominion status during WWII, he was still largely sidelined by the mass nationalist movements that dominated the freedom struggle throughout the 1930s and 1940s.

**** ****

WORLD WAR-2 and **QUIT INDIA MOVEMENT**:

Sastri's moderate, cooperative stance during World War II, including refusal to resign from the **British War Committee** and opposition to the **Quit India** movement, placed him at odds with the dominant Congress leadership and radical nationalists.

The "*War Committee*" during World War II was constituted by the British Government in India. It was mandated to coordinate and oversee the Indian contribution to the Allied war effort. This committee was part of the administrative and consultative mechanisms set up by the colonial government to manage military, strategic, and resource mobilization issues during the war.

Sastri's role in the *War Committee* was as a member representing Indian interests from a moderate, constitutionalist perspective. He did not hold a formal military rank but served as a senior political advisor and elder statesman. His participation reflected his pragmatic support for India siding with Britain during the war while advocating orderly constitutional progress and **opposing radical civil disobedience** such as the **Quit India Movement**. Sastri's presence on the committee was part of his broader role as an experienced diplomat and political moderate engaged in advising the British government and advocating Indian concerns within legal and constitutional frameworks.

Sastri made no secret at all that he considered the **Quit India movement of 1942** as an impossible demand that could lead to anarchy and appreciated the difficulties faced by Britain in the war. Sastri blamed India's problems more on Indian disunity than British policy and **maintained that British rule was "*providential*"** as part of India's political evolution. Thus, he chose to remain on the *War Committee* as a moderate voice supporting dominion status and constitutional progress, rather than withdrawing in protest or radical opposition.

There is no specific record of who exactly demanded that Sastri resign from the *War Committee*, but it can be inferred that the more radical elements of the *Indian National Congress* and *Quit India Movement* supporters would have expected loyal Indian leaders to resign in protest of British rule during the war. Sastri's steadfast refusal to resign set him apart from the Congress leadership and the mass nationalist activism of the period.

V. S. Srinivasa Sastri did experience thus a form of political alienation during the later years of the Indian freedom struggle, especially as the mass nationalist movements led by Gandhi and Nehru became increasingly dominant. However, the relationship between Sastri and Gandhi was marked by mutual respect and personal friendship despite their sharp political differences. Gandhi even continued addressing Sastri as his *"elder brother"* in their correspondences and praised his qualities. Their personal rapport remained warm.

**** ****

Sastri himself however did express a nagging sense of melancholy caused by his political isolation in the late 1930s and early 1940s, lamenting that Indian liberals were *"not wanted"* in the political landscape dominated by radical nationalism. This nuanced picture is reflected in biographies and archival letters showing Sastri's dignified but melancholic withdrawal from frontline nationalist politics in the 1930s and 1940s.

Below is a mere sampling of such letters of Srinivasa Sastri. They all truly reflect the mood of subdue and melancholy that was gradually creeping upon him in his advancing years but which he yet bore with stoicism and, in fact at times, with remarkably good humour. With his good friend, the outstanding legal and Constitution luminary, **Alladi Krishnaswamy Aiyar**, Sastri shared his gnawing sense of isolation but then at the same time also pulled Alladi's legs, playfully shaming him for being overly preoccupied with mundane and quotidian task in his humdrum life and for neglecting to show even due gratitude to his *"long-suffering"* spouse!

TO ***RAO BAHADUR A. KRISHNASWAMI AIYAR***

POONA**: **31st March 1935

Dearest Friend,

This note is several days behind, but there is no more to write for that reason. Life is reduced to routine for me and one day is so like another, I ask myself why to prolong.

You come frequently into my thoughts-stooping and looking at your own sandals, which you drag with an effort, the ancient blanket resting on the shoulder with accustomed repose, the fingers of the right hand tracing queer lines on the heedless air, the head no longer poised firmly, but thrown forward and a wee bit sideward, as if too heavy with borrowed cares and adopted tasks, and the mind—ah, that mind! who shall sort its contents? May be the most suitable transport of a patient from Guindy (a suburb of Madras) to the hospital, maybe a word of unfelt anger to the school contractor, maybe the supply of a missing link in the chain of evidence for a trumpery small-cause suit to which a cousin or a nephew of an old friend is a party, maybe some subtle flattery by which a simple official could be wheedled into forgetting restrictive bye-laws. … Good honest items everyone: but does it strike you ever that others may do them just as well as you, and that if they were not done so well, the world would not be the worse the least bit?

Why not listen two hours daily to the melting "Tevaram" (Tamil sacred hymns of Saivite scriptures) of a half-starved "Andi" (anchorite), helping the puzzled intelligence of a neighbour with pregnant comments on the vocables and allusions? Why not get an old "shastri" (Vedic priest) to chant the Upanishads or expound the Gita, now and then startling him by questions suggestive of the limitation of rishis or the unbridled exegetical ingenuity of (Adi) Sankara?

And why not, I ask twice, why not spend a quiet hour at home, submitting to the just reproaches of a long-suffering partner, from whom so much has been exacted but to whom so little has been given? Believe me always your saucy, but reverent and worshipful,

V.S. SRINIVASAN

**** ****

The spectre of World War-2 breaking out in Europe disturbed Sastri and even aggravated his personal mood of depression. Sastri was admired by the noted Kannada poet and prolific **Sahitya Akademie Award** winning writer, **"DVG", D.V. Gundappa** (1887-1975). In a letter addressed to DVG, Sastri's mental state of anxiety can be truly fathomed:

To: ***Mr. D.V. GUNDAPPA***

MYLAPORE: 4th October 1938

My dear Gundappa,

Born in 1869, I am only 69 now. That is, I have completed 69 years. When Sept. 22 comes round in 1939, I should be a septuagenarian, if....

The world is going mad. I never was so perplexed in my life as now. Do I want peace or war? Peace.

Then why am I not pleased? Because of the extinction (it will be that soon) of Czechoslovakia. Did I expect peace in a Hitler-ridden world without some iniquity? If I did, I was a fool. Much as I disliked Halifax when he said: 'Peace is at this juncture greater to the world than justice', I don't dislike him nearly so much now. Peace is something more tangible, at least in its negative aspects, than justice, and far more clearly discernible. Who would sacrifice a clear tangible end for a mere abstraction which means different things to different nations and different individuals? This peace, however, cannot last long. Some people would ask: "Since we must fight someday, why, not now? it may be better now than tomorrow."

The answer is that of the doctor in the case of the dying man. He can't say: "Since the patient is sure to die in three days, why not finish him now? So much bother is saved."

The idea is God's ways are inscrutable. Nothing is certain. If we gain time, who knows? Mankind may change its ways, the nations may learn the wisdom of peace, and all quarrels will yield to reason.

Let Chamberlain (then British Prime Minister) have the peace prize and give a share of it to Daladier (French Radical-Socialist centre-left politician, then Prime Minister of France in 1933, 1934) and to Mussolini (then Italian Prime Minister) and to (Adolf) Hitler himself. Benes (then Czech politician and statesman who served as the president of Czechoslovakia in 1935-1938) is to have nothing but the world's pity and scorn.

My brain is now feeble and fitful in its work, and I daren't trust its verdict. But there will be a few more wars before the reign of peace begins. Then the earth and its peoples will be very different from what they are to-day.

Affectionately yours

V. S SRINIVASAN

**** ****

The most poignant of his letters expressing the utter sense of isolation and loneliness he felt at being marginalized by the mainstream of politics in India in that long period was the one Srinivasa Sastri wrote to a dear and personal friend to whom he truly opened out his heart and vented feelings:

To **Mr T. N. JAGADISAN**:

COIMBATORE: ***7th June 1941***

My dear Jagadisan,

A few years ago, I used to plague myself with examination of my past and contemplation of the great chasm between what might have been and what was....

Now I have a solace, but you will he surprised, perhaps shocked, to know of it. What would it have signified to the world, I ask, if I had realized my possibilities to the full ?

True pessimism, you say. Stern reality, I rejoin.

Pray do not imagine I have a grievance against the world. I have none. On the contrary, the world has been kind; not only tolerant, but generous. A diffident, ungrasping man is generally at a disadvantage; but luck has been friendly to me. Good things have sought me, occasionally found me timid and hesitant. I have not actually run away from such opportunities; conscience-stricken and scared, I have sat up and done my duty. ***But I was never eager, not at all ambitious and sadly deficient in the quality of adventure. If I sat at the table of the mighty, I was content to eat what I needed. I did not shout for the viands and costly wines and gorge myself.***

To speak the truth, I was every moment weighed down by the feeling that I had strayed out of bounds. I never settled down where I was stationed, but sat on the edge of the chair, ready to vacate if stared at questioningly by any steward.

Conquerors must be made of sterner stuff.

Affectionately yours

V. S. SRINIVASAN

**** ****

Despite his relations with Gandhi remaining as warm and affectionate as ever, still there was no doubt that his deep and wide political differences with the Mahatma's politics and leadership did at times chafe and even rankle Srinivasa Sastri. In one of his letters to another friend, and in a moment of rare candour, Sastri gave voice to all his suppressed bitterness:

To Mr A. V. THAKKAR

R. S. PURAM, COIMBATORE: *12th September 1941*

My dear Thakkar

You will have seen my statement on Churchill's declaration. He is a powerful man, now all powerful and puffed up. India can tackle him, if she is united, practical-minded, long-sighted. Jinnah has tied himself up into a tangled knot. He is paralysed. Gandhiji can shake himself and strike a new line but he too for the moment is in perverse company and wedded, like the I.C.S. (Imperial Civil Service bureaucrats) of old time, to prestige and consistency. These are the shibboleths of party but the ruin of the nation. ***He can't give up his morals and Ahimsa, but he can stand aside and give a chance to an alternative policy.*** *Stark abdication, publicly announced, may cause a panic and do terrible harm. But acquiescence in another line of approach is feasible. He is aware of it.* ***However, I am impotent and have no business to advise. So, I shut up.*** *Love.*

Yours affectionately

V. S. SRINIVASAN

**** **** ****

Chapter 10
An "Ahimsa" purer than Gandhi's....

Srinivasa Sastri's melancholia that clearly arose from a general sense of being cut off from mainstream political life in India during the years leading up to the Indian National Congress's **QUIT INDIA Movement** -- and thereafter too until his death in 1946 – was worsened by declining health.

It is documented that Sastri suffered from acute *angina pectoris* from around 1923, which handicapped him for the rest of his life, a fact that he acknowledged implicitly through his lifestyle and writings, though no extensive personal medical diary is publicly cited.

Sastri wrote and spoke about his delicate health condition which he suffered for many years. In detailed biographical recollections, it is described how he experienced chest pain and physical weakness, especially in his later years. For instance, during one episode of severe attack of chest pain, those around him noticed his distress and efforts to manage the pain with calm perseverance. He even expressed a wish to listen to devotional music during his painful moments, reflecting a spiritual and composed approach to his ailment.

To his close friends, Sastri seemed to have at times lamented in conversations about the time-consuming care of his frail body, which he felt interfered with his work and productivity. He spoke candidly about the demands of maintaining his physical health due to his heart condition while continuing his intellectual and literary pursuits.

Sastri's mood of loneliness is reflected in brief autobiographical essays in Tamil language that he penned in the year 1942. Here below are a few Tamil passages from his book in ***'மீண்டும் வாழ்ந்தால்'*** (*Meendum Vazhndhaal*, "If I Live Again") along with English translations. Clearly, they reflected his utter disenchantment with politics and the fading relevance of his moderate liberal ideals and that of his very own conception of "*ahimsa*" which he envisioned as the upholding of Non-violence not only in thought, word and deed, but more importantly, in demonstrably Dharmic terms too and which is what, he felt, rendered his philosophy of *Ahimsa* purer perhaps than Mahatma Gandhi's or Nehru's?

"நான் ஒரு தாழ்ந்த மண்ணின் குண்டு போலவே, என்னையும் எழுப்பக்கூடியது எதுவும் இல்லை. இந்திய லிபரல் பாகுபாடு முற்றிலும் முடிந்துவிட்டது — சில வருடங்களாக இங்கு உயிரின் ஊற்றே இல்லாமல் மௌனமாகக் கருகிக் கொண்டிருக்கிறது. இத்தகைய உலகில் நம்மை அவர்கள் விரும்பமாட்டார்கள் என்பது தெளிவாக தெரிகிறது."

"I am like a clod of miserable earth, which nothing can galvanize. The Indian Liberal Federation is entirely dead — for several years now it has been quietly dissolving without any sign of life. In such a world, it is clear that we are not wanted."

"சிறு ஒரு பண்பாட்டுக் கூட்டமைப்பாக இருந்த இந்த லிபரல் கூட்டமைப்பு, இப்போது இயல்பாகவும்

அமைதியாகவும் சிதறி கரைகிறது. அதற்கு ஏதாவது சிறப்புக் கடைசி நிகழ்ச்சி வேண்டுமோ என்று நினைப்பதில்லை."

"This Liberal federation, which was once a small cultural association, is now naturally and quietly dispersing and dissolving. I do not think any special final ceremony is needed for it."

"என்னுடைய சிந்தனைகள், உயிரின் ஈடுபாடுகள் இப்போது குறைந்து வருவதற்குச் சாத்தியமான காரணங்கள் அவ்வளவாகவே உள்ளன. நான் அரசியலில் இருந்து அங்கேப் பின்பற்றிப் போனேன், ஆனால் இதயத்தில் அந்தப்போதும் மற்றவர்களுக்கு காட்டிய கண்ணோட்டம் அதுவே தொடர்கிறது."

"My thoughts and life's engagements have increasingly diminished for understandable reasons. I have withdrawn from active politics, but the outlook I always held toward others continues in my heart."

**** ****

The passages above reveal Sastri's bleak sense of political isolation and resignation as his moderate political vision became marginalized during the rise of radical nationalist leadership like Jawaharlal Nehru's. They express his quiet acceptance of the fading role of liberal constitutionalism in the Indian independence movement, reflecting his deep disenchantment with the political climate of his time.

Amidst the political turmoil and moral turbulence of his times, Rt. Hon'ble Srinivasa Sastri may, deep inside his heart, have felt that he had consigned himself to the wrong side of History... But then not once did he ever show weakness of will in ploughing his own lonely furrow; nor ever did he waver in his convictions. The Bengali poetic line of **Rabindranath Tagore** *"Jôdi Tor Dak Shune Keu Na Ase Tôbe Ekla Chôlo Re (**"If no one responds to your call, then go your own way alone**"* was his inward motto.

Both V. S. Srinivasa Sastri and Rabindranath Tagore, in fact, were representative figures of ***classical liberalism*** in the Indian context—championing individual freedom, rational inquiry, pluralism, dialogue across cultures, and constitutional progress. Tagore considered Sastri "***the greatest ambassador and interpreter of Indian culture in the West***"—a reflection of their shared cosmopolitan, liberal outlook and mutual admiration in intellectual circles.

Thus, to Sastri alone perhaps amongst all other politician-diplomats of his generation, would the three verses below in the "***Elegy Written in a Country Churchyard***" of the English poet, **Thomas Gray**, most befit:

" Full many a gem of purest ray serene
The dark unfathom'd caves of ocean bear:
Full many a flower is born to blush unseen,
And waste its sweetness on the desert air.

Here rests his head upon the lap of Earth
A youth, to Fortune and to Fame unknown;
Fair Science frown'd not on his humble birth
And Melancholy mark'd him for her own.

Large was his bounty, and his soul sincere;
Heaven did a recompense as largely send:
He gave to Mis'ry all he had, a tear,
He gain'd from Heaven, 'twas all he wish'd, a friend.

**** ****

In his own words seen above, Sastri had said that although he had *"withdrawn from active politics"*... his *"outlook held towards others"* nonetheless continued unaffected in his heart. In other words, neither did his sense of political isolation nor his cold-shouldering by his colleagues in the freedom movement, nor his frail health condition, broke his indomitable spirit that made him still a man whose erudite opinions and awesome moral presence could never be ignored at any time... not even by the Viceroy of the British Government nor by Mahatma Gandhi.

From his home in Mylapore, Madras, Sastri often took up cudgels on behalf of his fellow-compatriots, Gandhi and Nehru, by writing strong, extremely articulate missives to the Government of India. Below are reproduced two of those brave, stinging yet polite and eloquent letters.

On **24th October 1943**, Sastri wrote to the British Viceroy in India **Lord Archibald Percival Wavell**. He was appointed and took office as Viceroy in June 1943, succeeding **Lord Linlithgow** who was the Viceroy during the earlier part of the year including the terrible Bengal famine for which Prime Minister **Winston Churchill** had been squarely responsible, as it came to light later. Lord Wavell served as Viceroy from 1943 to 1947.

To **H. E. THE VICEROY**

Your Excellency,

*My heart misgives as I think of the many delicate and intricate tasks that await you. We have been assured of your resolution, independence of judgement and liberal outlook. That is satisfactory, but not sufficient. Your training must have exalted obedience high above all other virtues and made you impatient of the slowness and caution of diplomacy and the compromises of parliamentary negotiation. Besides, the Indian politician's attitude, suspicious and soured by generations of deferred hope, may be a puzzle and soon become your despair. Can you look beyond the narrow circle of official advisers and invite to your aid the patriotism of the land, which now is held at arm's length, because it will not neglect Indian honour and Indian welfare? Can you see, in men and women branded as disloyal, eager colleagues in the service of India and of the Empire? Anxious eyes and ears from every corner will be directed towards New Delhi to find out whether you " **weigh well**" and not merely **"maxwell."***

Sastri's delightful punning on the name of the British Viceroy's name of "*Wavell*" with "*weigh well*" and "*maxwell*" could not have gone unnoticed or grudgingly admired even by the British!

"Anxious eyes and ears from every corner will be directed towards New Delhi to find out whether you 'weigh well' and not merely 'maxwell'" was Sastri's pointed and brilliant play on words referencing **Sir Reginald Maxwell**, who was the Home Member of the Government of India at that time.

In historical context, Sir Reginald Maxwell was a prominent British official involved in the administration and political affairs, often associated with repressive measures during the period. Sastri's phrase *"weigh well"* meant the Viceroy's actions was going to be judged on their merit and effectiveness (i.e. how well he performed and carried weight in his role), rather than being merely another "*Maxwell*"—alluding to Sir Reginald Maxwell's controversial reputation.

The trenchant literary usage of a pun by Sastri was a veiled advice to the Viceroy to abandon the repressive policies often linked to Maxwell. The phrase, in fact, captured the expectation of Indian leaders and the public during a critical period in 1943, awaiting whether the Viceroy would act justly and wisely amid the intense political unrest and demands from Indians following *the Quit India* movement.

Thus, "*weigh well*" contrasted the idea of true leadership and responsibility with the negative connotations surrounding "*Maxwell*" — the name that symbolized heavy-handed, unjust governance. This was Sastri's trademark way of conveying subtly yet sharply how large the political stakes for the British administration in India at the time were and how fraught with risks for Lord Wavell's own helmsmanship.

In the same acerbic but polite vein, and in the same letter, Sastri continued with another trenchant but veiled criticism of **Leopold Charles Amery**, the Secretary of State for India and Burma from 1940 to 1945 under **Prime Minister Winston Churchill**. Amery was known for his deep interest in British India and the British Empire and often clashed with Churchill on Indian policy. He was born in India and was fluent in Sanskrit, giving him a unique connection to India among British officials of that era)

"*I will ask leave to say another word. The Secretary of State has declared, I fear, that British Parliamentary democracy may not suit India and advised us to invent a new type of popular government for ourselves. I am not known to be an uncharitable critic; but I find it hard to believe that he can be serious. What Britain does not know and has not tried, she cannot conscientiously recommend to a people less experienced or guide them in operating it. For a century and a half, we have studied British institutions and admired them. When Mr Montagu (i.e.* **Edwin Montagu,** the Secretary of State for India from 1917 to 1922) *framed his proposals* (for reforms of British Rule over India) *and published them for criticism in India, some of us would have preferred an* *unremovable executive* (i.e. a Presidential form of government). *I was among these. But he was all for the system of "ins" and "outs" and the majority of our leaders were attracted by the excitement and struggle incidental to recurring trials of parliamentary skill and strategy.*

For twenty years and more we have practised it and become used to it. To pronounce us unfit now and send us about in quest of another plan is to hold up things indefinitely, to strew the land with apples of discord and create such confusion as to imperil the constitutional progress so far achieved. If it was intended to punish us for venturing to look forward to furthering progress in the same direction, Mr Amery's advice would become intelligible.

Before we become much older, however, his attempt will encounter the fate of Canute's command to the sea. Not in these days can a nation's freedom be denied or delayed with impunity.

Yours sincerely

V. S. SRINIVASAN

Sastri's reference to *"Canute's command to the sea...."* is so very apt indeed to describe the then prevailing political situation of rising and even militant spirit of Indian Nationalism in the country and to which he was drawing the Viceroy's special attention. It was a proverbial reference to the legend in modern politics at that time in world affairs when allusion to *"King Canute's arrogance"* of "*attempting to stop the tide*" was a dire warning to all mighty empires of the world.

King Canute of England (*1016-1035 CE* reign) set his throne by the seashore and commanded the incoming tide to halt and not to wet his feet and robes. Yet "*continuing to rise as usual [the tide] dashed over his feet and legs without respect to his royal person"*. Then the king leapt backwards, saying: *'Let all men know how empty and worthless the power of kings is, for there is none worthy of the name, but He whom heaven, earth, and sea obey by eternal laws.'* "He then hung his gold crown on a crucifix and never wore it again *"to the honour of God the almighty King."*

**** ****

At the conclusion of the Second World War, the British Government became very enfeebled, and it realised that its grip over its colonial rule in India was slipping away and would soon have to give way sooner or later.

Her Majesty's Government thus organised what was called a series of conferences called **"The Peace Conference"** in London. Leading Indian political leaders were expected to participate in those round-table *Peace Conferences* to deliberate upon and put forward ideas for shaping India's post-war future, influencing global peace settlements, and pressing for Indian self-determination.

Sastri advocated that Mahatma Gandhi, being recognized as the world's foremost apostle of peace, should participate in those international efforts directed at negotiating peace with the British and India's status after the war.

Gandhi, however, refused to participate in the main international Peace Conferences due to his deep distrust of the British government's motives and process. He saw the Conferences not as genuine efforts to resolve India's political aspirations, but as British devices to divert attention away from the real colonial objectives of the Empire and perpetuate division among Indian communities—especially over communal questions (*Hindu*, *Muslim*, and *Dalit* interests). Gandhi felt that such conferences would not deliver real independence and that his presence could be used to falsely signal Indian endorsement of a British-driven process and agenda. He also believed his efforts were best directed at mass movements and local negotiations, rather than at fora he felt did not respect India's fundamental right to self-determination.

Sastri was dismayed by Gandhi's stubborn rejection of the British Government initiatives to hold the **Peace Conferences** as a prelude to eventual transfer of power to Indian leadership. In a passionate letter dated **October 24, 1943,** Srinivasa Sastri once again expressed his deep misgivings and disappointment over the Mahatma's political stance and tried to persuade him to change his mind. The letter --- one of the last few ones he sent to Gandhi --- was written in Sastri's inimitably eloquent style. But it is not without significance to note, that departing from his old habit of addressing Gandhi in all his letters as "*Dear Brother*," Sastri in this letter addressed him as "*Dear Mahatma!*" That departure told a story of the imperceptible estrangement that had imperceptibly crept into the relations between the two kindred souls.

FROM: V. S. SRINIVASAN

TO MAHATMA GANDHI

Dear Mahatma,

I pen these words in anguish. The days are hard for our motherland. P, would I know how you feel so that no random words of mine might add to the wretchedness and desolation which fill every minute of your life. Bear with me once more. At similar crises before, it has been my unenviable lot to address you with the harshness of unheeding truth but in accents of love.

The people of India, for whom you have slaved these thirty years as no one has done, lie prostrate in the deadly grasp of hunger, destitution and stark despair. A dismal sense of frustration oppresses them like a nightmare. Their trust in you, however, is the same, if possible, tenderer and purer for your sufferings and sorrows.

Promising plans are promising only so far as you may work them out. Proposals from any quarter are canvassed, but only so long as the execution stage is not reached; then they ask for you and speculation stops.

*Officials in their way and for their reasons, unofficial in their way and for their reasons, all alike turn to you. Only on half a dozen occasions have human hearts yielded themselves up in such complete thrall to one without birth, beauty of form, possessions, force of arms or honours to distribute. Every true Indian is proud that he can call you his fellow-countryman, and those that you have honoured with your friendship are among the blessed ones of their generation. Being one of these, I have used my privileged position now and then to remonstrate against the way you have allowed the doctrine of "**ahimsa**," of which you are the unanointed apostle, to be muddled in its application to the work of the Congress. Your answer is that you always meant to employ it in the furtherance of national aims and could not help the lapses. You add too, with humility all your own, that you are not a saint strayed among politicians, but a politician appearing like a saint and not to be judged by the highest standards. I am, however, unreconciled and own to a feeling of grief that one so near the summit of purity should not reach it.*

Dear brother, an opportunity has come, the like of which never was and never will be for generations. At the ensuing ***Peace Conference****, which may meet sooner than most people expect, the affiliated nations will seek ardently for brave and honoured advocates of justice, equality and brotherhood without distinction of race, colour or religion. You must be there. Who, if not you?*

War must be banished for ever from the earth and all possibility of its recurrence provided against so far as it can be provided against by human foresight. Would you he missing on that supreme occasion? No, a thousand times No. Pacifism, non-violence, ahimsa whenever and wherever these words are pronounced, the name of Gandhi will occur to the minds of people all over the earth. What should keep you from bearing irrefragable witness to the truth that you have ever cherished in your heart, the truth that must resound through the ages when your body has perished? After several humiliations due to association with earthly causes, the hour of exaltation approaches you.

I see you, Great Soul, in a vision of glory, go up the Mount of Expectancy of a weary, waiting world, raise high the right hand of blessing, and solemnly utter the word which is in all hearts, and which comes full of hope and full of meaning from your inspired lips.

Come, then, bestir yourself. Not a day should be lost.

There is so much to do before civilised administration can be restored and competent authorities in the provinces and at the Centre can be formed with national aims and appropriate means for the choice of delegates through whom the soul of India can speak to the rest of the world. Don't say you are not free. You can be free, if you but realise that you are waited for. Your last movement has not borne the fruit that you wished. Admit what everybody sees. No hesitation need be felt in recognising facts. You yield, no doubt. But you yield to Fate and not to man.

Stoop and conquer. Many a hero before you has done so and many a hero after you will do so. Let us consult the ***Ramayana****, a book which we revere alike. It counsels against the single aim and the single strategy. A good general should vary them. These are the words of* ***Hanuman****, whose aid all Hindus invoke before beginning great enterprises:*

"No single plan is adequate to achieve even a small aim. Only he can succeed in his purpose who adopts different plans in different circumstances."

Yours affectionately

V. S. SRINIVASAN

**** ****

Srinivasa Sastri's referencing specifically the ***Ramayana*** in what might perhaps have been one of his very last few letters to Mahatma Gandhi now perfectly sets the stage for us to segue to examining the great love for **Maharishi Valmiki's** "*itihaasa*" that Sastri truly cherished; and also the great erudition in it that he went on to display through his "**Lectures on the Ramayana**" which, in later years in his life, made him so famous.

**** **** ****

Chapter 11
Living for the love of Valmiki and Shakespeare

In the sunset years of his life --- i.e. the *early* and *mid-1940s* --- Srinivasa Sastri's physical and mental health remained beleaguered. His angina attacks came upon him suddenly and not infrequently. They caused him excruciating chest-pain and breathlessness. In those days in contrast to the present day, medical research had not yet discovered miracle drugs and wonder-pharmaceuticals to attenuate the physical distress caused by cardiac ailments. Also, the continued marginalisation of Sastri by the then political leadership of the Indian Freedom struggle movement (Gandhi, Nehru, Patel and Rajaji at the forefront) also made him at times feel mentally distraught.

Sastri however had many other interests, pastimes and passions in life from which he drew tremendous strength and *joie de vivre*: *books, literature, religion, Carnatic music* and a very affectionate and *close-knit family support-network* that provided him constant emotional solace. His wife, siblings, sons, daughters and extended family of many loving grandsons and grand daughters were always beside him. If ever he found the atmosphere in Mylapore, Madras, getting a little depressive, he was able to move on, go and spend quality time with his extended family living in other salubrious and quieter towns and cities such as Coimbatore and Bangalore. In those tranquil family surroundings Sastri was able to devote his time to the deepest passions in his life --- reading great literature, discussing books, having lively conversations with visiting friends and admirers, giving little talks on many a subject, listening to music and if nothing else to do, then simply indulge himself in personal reflections.

DVG (**D.V. Gundappa**, the prolific Kannada litterateur who was Sastri's friend and admirer) in a biography, wrote about Sastri's lifestyle during these sunset years in a charming pen-portrait (S*econd essay in D V*

Gundappa's magnum-opus ***"Jnapakachitrashaale"*** *(Volume 6) –* ***"Halavaru Saarvajanikaru"***:

QUOTE:

V.S. Srinivasa Sastri's daily routine in Bangalore was as follows: He got up before 7 in the morning and visited Lal Bagh. He would sit on the shore of the lake or on a bench in the garden. If he had an article in mind, he would dictate it, and it was my duty to write it down. This would usually go on for about half an hour or forty-five minutes. There were deer housed in front of the place where we usually sat down. He was very eager to see the deer ruminating grass and walking around in the enclosure. He would recite the poem – ***'romanthamākurvati'*** *from the* ***Śākuntalam*** *(of* ***Kālidāsa****) as he watched the deer. He walked around slowly. It was also my duty to stop him from walking very fast and to slow his gait down. At times, when he had lost himself in talking to me, he unconsciously accelerated his gait. If he met someone on the way who he could converse with, his speed of walking would go even further up. I had been told that I was to stop him from doing so.*

*As we took strolls in Lal Bagh different topics would come up for discussion. We often went by the mādhavī creeper present in the garden. He would see that and quote - "****Kṣāmakṣāmakapolam****..." from* ***Śākuntalam****. He would explain how to split the words, parse them and the summary of the poem. He spoke at length about the meaning of the verse. His manner of speaking itself was a huge treat for our ears and hearts. As he explained the meaning, he often quoted phrases and sentences from Sanskrit literature. At times, it turned into a monologue completely in Sanskrit and went on for a few minutes.*

We had many such lively conversations during our morning walks and returned home by nine in the morning. By then, the day's newspaper would have arrived. Sastri would go through the headlines that he felt were important and described their content to me. Discussions usually followed during and after his reading of the newspaper. This went on until eleven. He then would have his meal and retire for a siesta.

I would go back to his place by three in the afternoon. By then, his wife Lakshmamma would also have got some free time. We all sat together and had some lively discussions.

*Sastri usually read out sections from the **Vālmīki Rāmāyaṇa**. His wife, Lakshmamma then would compare what Vālmīki had said with the same sections from the Tamil poet **Kamban's Rāmāyaṇa.** She was more familiar with Tamil literature. A conversation regarding the beauty in both poems would ensue. Their study of the Rāmāyaṇa proceeded in a relaxed manner.*

*"Lakshmi! Read out what Kamban has written in the context of this incident. Let me hear it out". Though Srinivasa Sastri often claimed it as an excuse, he did not lack knowledge about the **Rāmāyaṇa in Tamil** at all. He went through the original Rāmāyaṇa in Sanskrit again and again and perhaps he did so all through the day. As he went through the original version of the Epic composed by Vālmīki, he grew curious to see how the other poets had described the same episodes. He would immediately call out for his wife. His beloved wife, Lakshmi would then read the Tamil version of the Rāmāyaṇa out loud and also compare it with the Tamil translation of Vālmīki's Rāmāyaṇa as rendered by **Srinivasa Iyengar**. Sastri would then examine in detail the manner in which **Kālidāsa** had presented the matter and how **Bhavabhūti** had creatively managed the same episode. Later, he discussed the same with friends who shared interest in the subject. I have been a witness to all this.*

By half past four or by five in the evening, Sastri's other friends visited him. On some days we headed out for a casual stroll to breathe in fresh air. In the beginning we rented a coach and travelled in it to inhale fresh air. Later on, one of our friends brought a car to take us around.

*Some evenings, he would hop onto his vehicle and go around the city, visiting places he thought were worth seeing. One such place was the **Sugrīva temple** located in Balepete. This was a unique thing for Sastri and had greatly kindled his interest. "Oh, He was a close friend of Śrī Rāma and helped him in his dhārmic activities. "Ah! Bangalore has people who remember Sugrīva!"*

During the early days of his stay in Bangalore, Sastri was very weak. How should he spend his time? I told him that I would bring a couple of books for him to read. Back then, I was going through the works of the Greek dramatist Sophocles. I was enthusiastic about the work – and I should admit that my enthusiasm was quite high. Being overly enthusiastic about somethings is one of my shortcomings. Sastri's reply was so impactful that I should note down for eternity –

"Why do I need to read anything new? My old Rāmāyaṇa and works of Shakespeare suffice!"

**** ****

Sastri's passionate love for " ***Valmiki Ramayana*** " was legendary indeed. In his last years, it was his veritable life breath, and it is what really kept him going despite physical and mental fatigue. His love for the "*itihaasa*" he expressed in these words with very intense feeling:

" ***The Ramayana I hold to be almost without a rival in the world's literature.*** *Whether we judge by the grandeur of the theme, by the variety of characters portrayed, by the tone of its idealism, of by the appeal that it makes to the devout heart, it ranks, amongst the noblest monuments of poetic genius. To those who cannot read it in the original, I would unhesitatingly recommend resort to translations. Even through media the narrative shines with rich brilliance".*

It was mainly thanks to Sastri's wholehearted advice to one and all, Indian or foreigner who "*cannot read it in the original*"... "*to resort to translations*" just so to be able to appreciate *"even through media, the narrative (that) shines with rich brilliance"*... which I say to myself, made me, in my own life and in my little forays into literature as an essayist, to embrace Sastri's recommendation.

It was thanks to Sastri's many scintillating essays on the *Ramayana* which I read with great admiration in my middle-aged years that I was able to creatively understand how the *"rich brilliance"* of the original work of Valmiki could be creatively enjoyed even in an English translation. Despite my knowledge of Sanskrit being no more than a smattering and limited to common usage of a dozen or more *Bhagavath Gita shlokas* and other verses from *Stotra* works of Vedantic Acharyas like **Adi Sankara, Sri Ramanujacharya** and **Sri Vedanta Desika**, I came to still marvel at Valmiki's Sanskrit as Sastri described it himself in his splendid peroratory style. Through the sheer brilliance of Sastri's own *Ramayana* exegeses in scintillating English language, I found myself gradually being able ... over the years ... to acquaint myself with the beauties of the *Maharishi's* Sanskrit poesy as seen through the eyes of Srinivasa Sastri. It never did surprise me, therefore, when later I read somewhere that Sir Winston Churchill and others were said to have been astonished at the *"beauty and power of Sastri's English,"* with the **Master of Balliol College**, ***A. L. Smith*** famously remarking, *"I never knew that the English language was so beautiful till I heard Sastri speak it".*

Personally, thus, Sastry's essays and lectures on India's greatest "*itihaasa*" brought me much closer to my own cultural roots than I felt I ever did before in life. When in 2016-17, I published my first book of essays ***"The Unusual Essays of an Unknown Sri Vaishnava"***, I made no secret of the fact in telling my readers upfront that many of the essays in my book dealing with themes from the *Ramayana* were largely influenced by Rt. Hon'ble Srinivasa Sastri. One short story, in fact, that I wrote and published in my book as a separate chapter titled ***"The Fourth Widow of Ayodhya"***, was a clear illustration of the deep spell of enchantment that Sastri's writings had cast upon my own.

**** ****

Sastri's undying love for Valmiki *Ramayana* was most definitely genetic in origin. It was a legacy of his own Vedic ancestry and hence he really did not have to make any great effort to carefully cultivate and nurture it in life.

Sastri was said to be able to quote large passages from Valmiki *Ramayana* verbatim with apparent ease. By his own account given in his Tamil autobiography, Sastri's prodigious memory was a matter of surprise even to himself! With no false modesty, and in all humility, he wrote that he could memorise with ease even passages from Milton' *Paradise Lost*:

"நான் முதலில் என்னை நினைத்தது போல சாதாரண மனம் கொண்டவன் அல்ல என்பதைக் காண நான் ஆச்சரியமடைந்தேன். பள்ளிக்கூட காலத்தில், மிக வெகு சீக்கிரமாகவே மில்டனின் Paradise Lost எனும் ஆங்கிலக் காவியம் எட்டாவது புத்தகத்துடன் நிறைவடையும் வரையிலும் என்னுள் நன்கு பதிந்து விட்டது. ஆச்சரியமானது என்னவென்றால், நான் படித்ததை நினைவில் வைப்பதற்கு சிலவேளைகளில் முயற்சி செய்யவே வேண்டாம் — அது தானாகவே மனத்தில் பதிந்து விடும்."

"I was surprised to find that I was not, as I had once thought, a person of ordinary memory. During my school days, Milton's Paradise Lost, right up to Book VIII, became firmly impressed upon my mind in a remarkably short span of time. What amazed me most was that I often didn't even have to make a

conscious effort to memorize — the words would settle into memory on their own."

Shankaranarayana Sastri, Srinivasa Sastri's father was a famous *paurāṇika* (bard, storyteller, raconteur). He delivered story-telling sessions on the *Rāmāyaṇa* in public. This is how Srinivasa Shastri developed great reverence and love for *Rāmāyaṇa*– it was something that had come down to him in his family. He then developed great scholarship in the work of Sanskrit poetry with the use of the English language. Sastri's ancestors, namely his grandfather, great-grand father and great-great-grandfather were scholars of *Veda* and *Vedānta*. They had taken to *yatyāśrama* (*sanyāsa*) in their old age and had attained *siddhi* (Ultimate goal, liberation).

Sastri was the eldest among his siblings. **Vasudeva Sastri, Narasimha Sastri** and **Ramaswami Sastri** were his younger brothers. Vasudeva Sastri was an inspector of the schools located in the Bellary region. He was very well educated. Narasimha Shastri worked at co-operative societies but was well educated too. Ramaswami Sastri worked as one of the Associate Editors of the *'Hindu'* daily newspaper and was erudite himself.

So, given the family background so steeped in Vedic scholasticism, Western erudition and Sanskrit learning, Sastri's love for the *Ramayana* came with his birth itself. And it exceeded the great love that he later in life cultivated for Milton and Shakespeare.

**** ****

Besides the *Valmiki Ramayana*, there were several other magnificent books and timeless classics that Srinivasa Sastri himself in one of his well-known essays listed out as being his all-time favourites.

*" **The Meditations of Marcus Aurelius** stirred me deeply by their utter sincerity and high-souled philanthropy. Curious as it may seem, **Tolstoy** took me captive by his **The Kingdom of God is within You.** I remember how the revelation came on me with a rush."*

Sastri also studied deeply **Herbert Spencer's** *Sociology* and **John Stuart Mill's** *Subjection of Women, On Liberty,* and *Three Essays on Natural*

Religion. He delighted too in the works of **T.H. Huxley's** *Evolution and Ethics.*

"The Iliad and the Ramayana can never die, so say our idealists. The Vedas, we swear, had no beginning and will have no end. Grand conceptions these, which it was vandalism to examine historically or appraise scientifically. To how few of the world's population of nearly two thousand million do they mean anything? In our own homes they have long ceased to be a direct means of enlightenment...

I would place in this category the great plays of ***Shakespeare*** *and moving orations like those of* ***Burke****. Who can escape the instruction of (Walter)* ***Scott's*** *novels or the edification of* ***George Eliot's****?* ***Wordsworth, Tennyson and Browning*** *go deeper down in your nature and shape it to finer issues."*

On **Victor Hugo's** *Les Misérables,* Sastri wrote:

"The story is one of the great epics of the world, the events and characters alike are cast in large moulds, and the sensitive reader is instructed, edified, scolded, exhorted, and by every possible means, shaped to be fit for a happier world than he now knows. Out of this vast storehouse of experience and history we carry away just so much wisdom as we are capable of. But there is no one, however exalted, however wise, however powerful, who can leave a study of this book without being summoned with the compelling majesty of supernatural law to the recognition of a more humane code of behaviour and a more altruistic sense of duty. If any one of my readers has not yet read this book, I bid him, with the authority that belongs to age and knowledge of the deeps and shoals of life, to get hold of a copy at once and benefit to the full by the treasures that its pages enshrine."

**** ****

In my opinion, the greatest gift the man who was called *"Silver-tongued Sastri"* gave to India is contained in the monumental literary legacy he left behind viz. **"The Lecture on the Ramayana."**

All other achievements for which Sastri was credited in the sphere of politics, international diplomacy, education and the arts all pale into insignificance in comparison to what he delivered as his *pièce de résistance,* the **Lectures**, which indeed were virtually his last bow too before his demise in 1946.

V. S. Srinivasa Sastri delivered his celebrated *Lectures on the Ramayana* in Madras (now Chennai) at the Sanskrit Academy. The series began on **5 April 1944** and concluded on **8 November 1944**. The initial lectures were part of a small, select gathering, but soon drew much larger crowds as word of their quality and insight spread through the city and region.

Sastri began the *Lectures* at the behest of his friends and only for the benefit of a small closely-knit circle. It all started in **T.R. Venkataramana Shastri's** house. As the people who attended the lectures started inviting their other friends and relatives to join them in the following days, the crowd kept growing. News about the lecture series spread through word of mouth. During a few of his lectures, the audience witnessed Sastri thoroughly immersed in the narratives of the Ramayana. At times, they saw him overcome with emotion as he spoke about the Epic and his voice choked. His eyes filled with tears, and he would go silent for a while. The audience that had gathered also then lost themselves in the lecture and felt that their life had found at last some meaning.

So enthralled was the audience by the experience of listening to Sastri's commentaries on the *Ramayana*, that a grand concluding ceremony for the series of lectures was organised for the audience to express its thoughts, gratitude and delight in going through the process. The people presented Sastri with a silver plate with letters from a Sanskrit *śloka* from the original *Rāmāyaṇa* embossed on it. The *śloka* was from the episode wherein **Rāma meets Āñjaneya** for the first time, and having got impressed with his manner of expression, Rama speaks words of appreciation. The audience was also, similarly, overwhelmingly impressed with Sastri's style of presentation and the *śloka* was thus so very relevant to the context.

संस्कारक्रमसंपन्नाम् अद्रुतामविलम्बिताम् ।
उच्चारयति कल्याणीं वाचं हृदयहर्षिणीम् ॥

saṃskārakramasaṃpannām adrutāmavilambitām ।
uccārayati kalyāṇīṃ vācaṃ hṛdayaharṣiṇīm ॥

D.V. Gundappa wrote: *"There is a school of thought in Indian literary aesthetics which considers Style as the Soul of Poetry – **"Rītirātmā Kāvyasya."** This holds true in case of Sastri's art of expression. His lecture was poetry, and the best part was his style of rendition."*

At least thrice in my life so far have I read Sastri's *"Lectures on the Ramayana"* in full and countless times have I turned to its pages by way of referencing. Each time I have experienced a different kind of delight while savouring the book. Every one of the thirty lectures is a masterly dissertation indeed on the *Ramayana* and the profound lessons on **Dharma** it is gem-encrusted with.

However, in my opinion, the most enlightening of all the 30 lectures is **Lecture No. 15.**

**** **** ****

Chapter 12
Lecture #15 of the "Lectures on the Ramayana"-1

Sastri felt politically marginalized by the rise of Gandhi and Nehru's mass movements. He expressed melancholy and resignation about the eclipse of moderate liberalism. *'I am a clod of miserable earth, which nothing can galvanise. Let me be,'*, he had written to a friend. His personal relation with Gandhi was respectful and affectionate despite political dissent. Nehru respected Sastri but politically differed sharply and no historian really knows if there was personal animosity towards him. Sastri's own mood was more one of sorrowful withdrawal and principled dissent rather than outright bitterness or rancour.

The feeling of being "*unwanted*" however did hurt Sastri acutely. He was aware that many within the *Indian National Congress* (INC) thought of him as a closet *Anglophile* whose real sympathies for British sense of colonial *constitutionalism* overrode Indian spirit of proud *nationalism.* And he also was only too conscious, again, that amongst more radical-minded quarters within the INC, a few people secretly even suspected his patriotism even though none did go so far as to regard him as an outright traitor to the cause of Indian freedom struggle. While all this indicated personal disappointment and sadness at his marginalization, Sastri still always maintained a dignified stance, continuing his intellectual and diplomatic contributions.

The only occasion however when Sastri's heart broke out and he felt the need to give voice to his long-suppressed feelings of hurt; pain and humiliation was during the period in Madras when he was delivering to his large Mylapore audience the ***"Lectures on the Ramayana."***

Throughout the thirty brilliant *Lectures* that he delivered --- over a span of seven long months between **April and November** of the year **1944** just as World War-2 was ending and India's own *Independence Movement*, after the near-abortive *Quit India agitations*, had wound down but was poised to revive again --- not once did Sastri in any of his grand narrations of the episodes and themes of the *Valmiki Ramayana*, stray from its faithful textual interpretations and character delineations into anything that could have been construed as veiled, related commentary insinuating upon the state of contemporary politics and social affairs of that time.

The Lectures instead were scrupulously focused only on the finest features and aspects of *Valmiki Ramayana* -- i.e. on its literary excellence, poetic beauty, aesthetic qualities, philosophical and moral inquiry of the most profound kind... Not once did the narrations descend to low-grade discourse about the sordid situations in run-of-the-mill politics prevailing then, nor about its polemics nor about the *dramatis personae* in it.

However, there was one departure... one glaring exception that stood apart from all the rest... It was in Sastri's **Lecture No. 15**.

In this exceptional *Lecture*, some deeply distraughtly feeling within him seemed to overcome Sastri and broke right through -- like the raging flash floodwaters breaching the great concrete wall of a high dam -- Srinivasa Sastri's reticence and characteristic self-restraint. It made him deliver a vociferous speech, pulling no punches and it indeed did go all out to reveal his disapprobation and utter disillusionment with the entire class of political leadership in India and the political climate it had created.

**** ****

In *Lecture No: 15* Sastri devoted himself to a detailed character study of **Vibheeshana**, the Lankan Prince.

This brother of the tyrant king, Ravana, as the story goes, relinquished his royal status, renounced ties with the Lankan nation and went seeking Lord Rama's asylum. Later he also threw in his lot with the latter's army that had gathered upon Lankan soil, waiting to launch a great war against King Ravana who had stubbornly refused to return to Rama the Lady Sita who he held hostage.

The dramatic dynamics of the whole Vibheeshana episode -- commonly known to all Ramayana scholars as "*Vibheeshana saranaagati sarga*-s" -- appears in the **Yuddha Kandam** of the *Ramayana.* The setting is the great War that is about to begin between Rama and Ravana. And the political fallout and churning that then consequently occurs inside the royal palace of Ravana --- in the form of tumultuous disagreements and mutual betrayals breaking out amongst brothers, uncles, cabinet ministers and advisors --- are all indeed so very redolent of the kind of widespread nasty politicking and venal political discourse we see in present-day India.

The entire *Yuddha Kandam* is filled, in fact, with the familiar theatre of disruptive, hate-filled, cynical and acrimonious scenes and script of modern-day politics. Accusations and counteraccusations of treason, deception, tyranny, moral turpitude, hubris and blood disloyalty are seen to fly thick and fast, back and forth with mutual recriminations being thrown at each other by brother against brother, kith against kin, amongst ministerial colleagues and between friends turning suddenly into foes....

The battleground atmosphere of the *Yuddha Kandam* is not just about military conflict alone. More significantly, such scenes in the epic also serve as metaphor for the greater battle of morals, of *Dharma* and *Karma*, the clash of ideologies, and for values at odds with culture. The role that the character of Vibheeshana plays in this *Kandam* is even today one of the most complex and enduring controversies in the entire "*itihaasa*." Vibheeshana was really the precursory model for Hamlet since his own moral predicament too was in the nature of that classic and often irreconcilable human dilemma: *"To be or not to be ... that is the question!"*

This roiling *Ramayana* episode seemed however to provide Sastri with the perfect platform from which he felt he could seek to put up a moral defence of the difficult choices he had made when he was in the thick of politics of India along with his guru **Gopal Krishna Gokhale** (***1866-1915* CE**) who had been a leading figure in it. It was because of the *Gokhale* brand and style of politics that Sastri had chosen to espouse and follow which was largely why, later on, he had come to be virtually ostracised and eventually excommunicated by the INC leadership under Gandhi and Nehru and had been left behind by them to languish in political oblivion.

Even though during the prime years of his career, Sastri was thought to be the most qualified of the entire lot of Congressmen and the most capable too amongst others who could fully engage, on behalf of the country, in international diplomacy at the highest levels not only with Imperial Britain but with the whole world, at the end, when the job was done and the INC changed course, the Party let it be known that it no further had any further use for Srinivasa Sastri.

Like Vibheeshana of the *Ramayana* had felt about his brother Ravana, Sastri too felt that he had been unjustly treated by his compatriots, Gandhi, Nehru, Patel and Rajaji, simply for remaining true and deeply committed to his very own philosophy of "*constitutional liberal-humanism*" that, in fact, had been also that of Gandhi's own one-time mentor, Gopal Krishna Gokhale, a leader whose principles were rooted in the tenets of *Dharma* and who fearlessly advocated opposition to the more popular but more radical philosophy of Gandhian "*satyagraha*" which as far as he was concerned was essentially nothing but *anarchist ahimsa.*

**** ****

What is clearly discernible in **Lecture#15** thus is that in the delivery of his oration, Srinivasa Sastri struck a vaguely autobiographical tone.

In the character of Vibheeshana, Sastri found the almost identical moral reflection of his own. The *Lecture* thus presents itself as a sort of auto-suggestive psychotherapy through which Sastri sought to deal with his own inner struggles in trying to overcome the deep and dormant trauma that political marginalisation from the centre-stage politics of the Indian Independence movement had caused and lacerated him.

If Ravana was the elder brother of the dissenting Vibheeshana, then perhaps Sastri was the dissenting younger brother to Mahatma Gandhi? And if Vibheeshana's renunciation of his elder brother and his embracing his adversary, Sri Rama, was morally defensible, how could Sastri's rejection of Gandhi's methods of "*satyagraha*" in favour of the much more moderate and constitutional forms of Gokhaleian political struggle be condemned as traitorous flirtation with *Anglophilia* and siding with the British?

In Sastri's own unexpressed opinion, the "*satyagraha*" of the Gandhi-Nehruvian type was perhaps *"crypto-himsa"* or, at best, say, a kind of dangerous "*hybrid-ahimsa*", which he feared would in the years ahead become the normative style of the general political culture, style and discourse in India. In his view, it was never going to instil true patriotism or true national spirit. And just because he had boldly articulated his fears did not mean that he should have been attacked *ad hominem* and cast out as some sort of a traitor to the cause of India's freedom from the British...

If one were to keep in mind all that is stated above, one certainly can get a much better understanding of the various issues that Srinivasa Sastri spoke about in **Lecture#15.** The tone and content of his speech might seem to some even today as a bit fulminatory. But the language --- even in its flights of purple rhetoric --- is yet ever so refined, cultured, reasonable and typically "*inoffensive*". And the trenchant messages so conveyed can hardly be ever faulted on any account ... certainly not for *bile, falsity, intemperance, exaggeration or self-righteous bromide.*

**** ****

The brilliant *Lecture#*15 contains profound observations indeed upon a very wide range of matters, political and philosophical *viz.: Conscientious objection, Patriotism, Treason, Nationalis*t *pride, Democracy, Political Dissent, Political civility, Temperance of speech* and last but not the least, the supreme importance of *mutual respect* that one human must always cultivate for another, no matter what idea, ideals, thought, feeling or prejudice separated them.

Today, as I read *Lecture#15* again -- for God knows how many times -- I am more than ever convinced that every word in it is an invaluable lesson in lofty ethics for our times. It is simply amazing to me how the *Lecture* delivered as far back as 1944 foresaw and predicted the pathetic way Indian politics would ultimately go... And how we in 2025, we are seeing with our eyes how Politics is conducted today and the way our politicians behave atrociously towards one another, both in public and in private. Sastri's own stirring words do make me recall the words of his own favourite English poet, *William Shakespeare:*

O judgment! thou art fled to brutish beasts,
And men have lost their reason...

O, what a fall was there, my countrymen!
Then I, and you, and all of us fell down...

**** ****

There is no other way for me but to extensively reproduce below, long and whole extracts from *Lecture#15* because any attempt on my part to present Sastri's speech in a paraphrase of my own will only end up marring, mutilating and mocking the mettle, the majesty and magniloquence of Rt. Hon'ble Srinivasa Sastry's masterful oratory.

**** **** ****

Chapter 13
Lecture#15 of the "Lectures on the Ramayana"-2

(*A 2025 Independence Day special*)

In **Mylapore, Madras**, on **July 19th, 1944**, Rt. Hon'ble Srinivasa Sastri delivered the fifteenth in his series of thirty sterling ***"Lectures on the Ramayana."***

Profoundly insightful observations were made in the course of the passionate speech upon a very wide range of matters, political and philosophical *viz.: Patriotism, Treason, Nationalist pride, Democracy, Political Dissent, Political civility, Temperance of speech* and, lastly but not the least, on the supreme importance of *mutual respect* that one human must always cultivate for another, no matter what idea, idealism, ideology, feeling or prejudice separated them.

**** ****

I happen to be writing this Chapter on the eve of the **15th of August 2025,** the **79th anniversary of India's Independence**, an occasion when great orations will be heard from the Red Fort in New Delhi and from the ramparts of Raj Bhavans and State Legislatures in State Capital cities right across India.

Great many lofty-sounding patriotic sentiments will be aired tomorrow in public, all as a matter of annual routine and ritual but very little genuine *national soul-searching* is likely to be seen anywhere. The pomp and pageantry of *Indian Independence Day* will all be over in a few hours of choreographed festivities and after the grand speeches have been made, the People will all go back to their homes and to their private burdens and challenges in daily life. The *politics of business* will go on as usual and so will the *business of Indian politics* too.

Many of Sastri's observations made in ***Lecture#15*** of the *"Lectures on the Ramayana"* way back on July 19, 1944, were made in the context of his expatiation on the episode and characterisation of Vibheeshana. Nonetheless, they resonate so strongly with us even today on the eve of ***August 15th, 2025,*** because what was said about India then holds equally good for India today. That the remarks Sastri made then are so relevant even today will become clear to us if we realise that the fundamental nature of Indian political and social life as he had described them to be in his own time has not changed much since then. If this assertion of mine sounds rather too jarring, too provocative or cynical, and is also prone to be, as I shudder to think, grossly misunderstood, perhaps the actual extracts of Sastri's oration from ***Lecture#15*** reproduced below will bear me out.

**** ****

ON DEMOCRACY

Democracy is certainly the best form of human governance that has yet been devised, but it wants to be served by brave men, by true men, by first-class men.

It stands liable ever to the greatest abuse at the hands of untried men who think that abuse is the staple of politics and hatred is the hallmark of patriotism.

This sermon has been drawn out of me partly because I think it is an evil of the day, which in India is of foreign origin and may well be eradicated, and partly because it accounts for the degradation to which the great name of Vibheeshana has been unfortunately subjected. If our politics were not what they are, if the word 'patriotism' has not been applied in the modern way, Vibheeshana's name would well have been pure and unsullied in our estimation.

**** ****

ON PATRIOTISM and NATIONALIST PRIDE

What is meant by Patriotism? I ought to be very careful in the words I use, for people who bring political bias in the listening of a leader interpret it in their own way, according to their predilections, not necessarily according to the words of the speaker or his real sense. Pray, let me be understood to say what I wish to say, not what you think I am saying.

I was going to say that patriotism is not necessarily a virtue of human character. It is an emotion. It is a high feeling, an inclination of the heart of a noble order, of an exalted character. But whether it works well or ill, whether the consequences of patriotism are good or bad, whether the country is served well by the patriot in the end, depends upon how the emotion is directed.

Take the love of the child in the mother. The mother would spill her blood, give her life for the child. What is there in the world which she would not do for the welfare of the child? But we all know how often mothers untrained to their task, not knowing the nature of children do not bring them up properly and even spoil their general health completely. However sincere, however loving, however devoted, however sacrificing she may be, the ignorant mother cannot bring up a child in proper ways. She herself, out of the excess of her love, becomes a source of the child's weakness, perhaps of its wickedness.

We see to what bad uses love may be put, and we know too how in times of famine and acute trouble, women, burdened with two or three children and not knowing how to find the day's bread for them, and thinking that they should put an end to their own lives, think that the necessary preliminary for that is that they should kill their own children. See where it leads. I am trying to point out that this noblest of all feelings, the love of her child, can lead a woman to the commission of deeds the very mention of which fills us with horror.

On the other hand, take a wise father or a wise mother who has read books on how the young should be protected and guarded from evil practices, who can teach them to love the noble and the sincere, and avoid what is likely to degrade. Think how strong a power for good in the life of our nation becomes the possession of a mother or father of that character.

So now you will see how I am justified in saying that even our strongest passions, our noblest emotions, are only to be welcomed to the extent that they are used for uplifting purposes by those in whose hearts they play a prominent part. Patriotism thus may be good, or it may be bad in its effects, however honourable a man's intentions may be. No man is born with all these good qualities.

If we want to examine their origin in human affairs, we shall find perhaps that they had a very simple physical origin, and from that physical origin, by gradual perfection of their associations, by gradual exaltation of the uses to which they are put, these moral ideas have become purer and purer, until now we think that the chief end and aim of education is to inculcate them in the young.

Allow me a few minutes to show how patriotism arose in human history. Patriotism is not today what it meant at first. At first patriotism was largely confined to tribes and communities. From being strictly limited to families and to little villages, it gradually extended and came to mean a kindly feeling, a love of our kinsmen, a love of our people.

*In our history, we have the **Kosalas**, the **Vaidehas** and communities of that kind. No one had a country or land or district of his own. He belonged to a certain tribe or community, whose welfare was to him a prime concern. Originally this community migrated in the land. People moved rapidly from one part of the land to another, and gradually this feeling was transferred to the land itself, until now, by long usage, the word 'patriotism' is applied much more commonly to a feeling concerning the country where we were born rather than to a feeling concerning the people to whom we belong. Now, that is the change that has come over the word 'patriotism'... From being communal or tribal, it gradually transferred itself to the country where these communities or divisions settled down permanently.*

**** ****

ON TREASON and TRAITORS

It is in this section of **Lecture#15** that we come across suggestive hints that Sastri, in the course of offering a stout defence of the character of Vibhishana in the *Ramayana*, might have been subconsciously also offering -- as much to himself as to his audience -- a veiled rationalisation and justification for the role he himself had played in the Indian freedom struggle.

In the passage quoted below, he conducts a sort of psychoanalysis of the character of Vibheeshana. But then, it was also a way to psychoanalyse himself by which he identified, in part, with Vibheeshana's character. Whether Sastri found the experience cathartic or therapeutic, or not, we will never, know for sure, of course.

Sastri, through the same process, had found a way of rationalising to himself why such sharp differences and divergences had arisen between himself and the INC under Gandhi and Nehru's leadership. His explanations for Vibheeshana's deep moral misgivings about Lankan politics in Ravana's time, in fact, may have served Sastri well in reflecting upon how he himself had to cope and come to terms with many conflicts that he had had to face in his own political career in India.

Vibheeshana had dissented with Ravana bitterly. And Sastri too had found himself dissenting from his elder brother Gandhi, not to mention his acolytes, Patel, Rajaji, Nehru *et al*, and it was mainly about the **Ends and Means** to be adopted in the fight for Indian Independence. While Gandhi did teach that the *means* are as important as the *ends*, Sastri's objection was that even noble ends could not justify methods that risked destabilizing society or weakening ethical respect for government and law. He was particularly troubled by Gandhi elevating mass suffering and imprisonment to a political virtue. He feared that it sentimentalized public policy and undermined rational discourse.

Sastri is noted to have regarded Gandhi as something of a *"philosophical anarch"*. To Sastri it seemed that Gandhi believed *Order could come out of Chaos...* and Sastri believed the exact opposite: *From chaos could come only more Chaos.*

To Sastri, Gandhi's *Civil Disobedience* was not any kind of high-minded political philosophy. It was at best a clever-by-half, innovative political non-violent guerilla tactic. Thus, from the chaos of *Civil Obedience* mass-movements in pre-independence India, Sastri feared, what would ultimately emerge could only be a motley, rambunctious, unstable or chaotic Democracy. Sastri viewed the masses as not yet ready, in terms of political discipline and education, to safely wield the power of governance through rule of law when Independence was attained. He saw only the great danger of emotional crowds replacing deliberative debate.

Sastri clung to espousing the way of **Gopala Krishna Gokhale**, his political guru viz. "*gradualism*" and "*constitutionalism.*"

It favoured gradual, evolutionary progress—step-by-step reforms—over mass agitation and popular upheaval. Gokhale had always said that deep-rooted social or political change had to be built patiently within existing frameworks, not imposed through extra-legal pressure or mass mobilization against the state. But Gandhi and Nehru had by then already jettisoned Gokhale's idealism and instead embraced the philosophy of *Satyagraha*, which Sastri was convinced, contained within itself the dangerous, viral seed of anarchic politics. It might, in the short-term, serve well the purposes of "*non-violent Civil Disobedience and Non-Cooperation*" politics but for the future of Indian nationhood in the years ahead, it meant only one thing: a political culture of chaos, indiscipline and social strife.

Through a masterly portrayal of Vibheeshana as a tragic, anti-heroic victim of vindictive, clandestine politics, Sastry juxtaposed himself in this *Lecture* along with that same *Ramayana* character, holding its portrayal up as one of unjust vilification by North India that had misread and misunderstood Vibheeshana altogether. In saying so, Sastri was subtly insinuating that despite he, a scholar-politician of no mean stature from South India, had been misunderstood and vilified by his more dominant, assertive colleagues from the North.

Even it were only a matter of pure literary conjecture that Srinivasa Sastri saw Vibheeshana as an allegorical metaphor for himself, the case made in the Lecture as defence for the moral choices the Lankan prince made seemed to be really made on his own behalf too.

Sisters and brothers,

In the opening days of ***1907****—thirty-seven years ago-there occurred an event in the political world of India, which will serve as a suitable introduction to my talk today. The famous* ***Dadabhai Naoroji Congress*** *had concluded, and the feeling of Congressmen generally was that the threatened split had for the time been averted and that our efforts should all be directed to its prevention next year. That, however, as you know, was not to be.*

After the ***1906 Congress*** *concluded, Mr. Gopal Krishna Gokhale, who had taken a prominent part in the proceedings, thought that the good work should be completed by a series of public talks in various parts of India, showing young people how wild talk about the severance of the British connection and about a thorough-going boycott of everything British might end in disaster. He toured through Upper India, and his first lectures had a very great effect, producing anguish in the hearts of those whose efforts to weaken the Congress had caused all the trouble.*

At that time Bengal was served by a famous daily newspaper called ***'Bande Mataram'****. Its editor was* ***Aurobindo Ghosh****. The first lectures had appeared in the press, and they were reported in full. We were all astonished one morning to read the editorial headed* ***"Exit Vibhishana"****. The idea was that Gokhale,* ***by declaring himself on the side of the British power and against the surging national movement,*** *had played the part, the odious part, that Vibhishana played when deserting his brother and going over to join Sri Rama on the other side of the water.*

I was naturally hurt very much by the reference to my master Gokhale, but I was still more hurt by the use of the name Vibhishana to signify a ***traitor****, I had been brought up to believe that Vibhishana was a* ***Bhakta*** *of the first order, that he was a noble character who might be held up to pious people as an example of devotion to* ***Dharma*** *and to those who practised it with sincerity.*

Was Vibhishana to be held up to public execration as a man who had abandoned a noble cause and exposed his kinsmen and his land to the perils of a foreign invasion? That anyhow was not the light in which I was trained to understand that character. And on enquiry I was much pained to learn that the name Vibhishana was used, generally speaking, in ***Upper India*** *to mean a* ***traitor, a betrayer of his national cause****. That opened up a great difference between North India and South India in the understanding of this great epic, the* ***Ramayana****. But I am glad my enquiries since then have proved that there is not that very great difference that I thought at that time was prevalent.*

There are many in South India who, for some reason, inflamed by the political feeling of the day, regard Vibhishana as a character to be held up to contempt and to odium; and there are in other parts of India many who hold the contrary opinion. Nevertheless, I think, if we were to take a census today, we should find more people inimical to the reputation of Vibhishana in Upper India than here.

**** ****

(*As an aside:*) ON VISHISHTADVAITA SOTERIOLOGY

In the course of this passionate speech, and right in the middle of this very same section in **Lecture#15**, Sastri also exhibited -- by way of a remarkable aside – his intimate knowledge of **Visishtadavaita** soteriology too!

As a *Sri Vaishnava* myself, when I first read the little passage below, I was wonderstruck by Srinivasa Sastry's catholicity and with what superb appositeness he had brought it to bear too as an allusion while weighing in with his redoubtable argument:

It appears to me a misfortune that a character in our greatest epic whom the Poet himself has held in the highest esteem and whom for centuries upon centuries India has regarded as an ideal devotee, a man who exemplified by whatever he did, according to the ***Visishtadvaitins****, in faithful reproduction, the various attributes and stages, one after another, of the progress of a* ***"prapanna"****, that a character of that high order should by any means be regarded by the politically inflamed people of the time as a character to be avoided, to be mentioned only with disapprobation.*

**** ****

Lecture#15 then proceeded further in the same vein with Sastri juxtaposing himself, very subtly, very suggestively in veiled if not cryptic manner, right beside the character-mould of Vibheeshana:

It seems to me to be a melancholy fact, and I cannot reconcile myself to it. I wish today, talking to an audience in sympathy with Valmiki and his general ideas, in sympathy with our great traditions, that Vibhishana should be possibly saved from his detractors, and presented to you in what I consider to be a correct light. I hold that Vibhishana was a good man according to the standards of his time and is a good man according to the standards of our time too. Let me make my meaning clear by devoting a part of the time this evening to an illustration of the chief elements of Vibhishana's nature.

In the above excerpt, in the line -- viz.; *"I wish today, talking to an audience in sympathy with Valmiki and his general ideas, in sympathy with our great traditions, that Vibhishana should be possibly saved from his detractors, and presented to you in what I consider to be a correct light"* -- if *Vibheeshana* were to be substituted with *Srinivasa Sastri*, a reader like me perhaps would tend to believe that Sastri was simply referring to himself.

**** ****

Sastri next proceeded to define who is a **Traitor**. He posed a classic rhetorical question to his audience. He held up to them a painting, as it were, that was a vivid contextual representation of the moral predicament, the horns of dire dilemma on which Vibheeshana in the **Yuddha Kandam** found himself impaled. His own situation, his own moral quandary with which Sastri had grappled with on the Indian political stage seemed to be vividly mirrored by Vibheeshana's predicament:

> *The first question that occurs to me is, who is a traitor? In common parlance today, a traitor would be one who betrays his country or his nation to the enemy who has invaded the country and makes war upon it. By extension, of course, it would apply to any politician or public worker who sets himself deliberately for private profit, or who, for the sake of title or for some such purely worldly considerations, sets himself against the efforts made by patriots for the liberation of their country.*

It is not very difficult to fathom who Sastri really had in mind when he stressed that the word "traitor" could "*by extension, of course, ... would apply to any politician or public worker who sets himself deliberately for private profit, or who, for the sake of title or for some such purely worldly considerations, sets himself against the efforts made by patriots for the liberation of their country."*

A new political-class and breed of people by then in Sastri's times had already emerged in India. It had begun flocking into the *Indian National Congress Party* and had begun dominating it. The Congress Party's future ethos was in the making and Sastri was clearly alluding to it.

**** ****

ON POLITICAL DISSENT, POLITICAL CIVILITY

The rousing, conscience-stirring words quoted below spoken by Srinivasa Sastri on this subject are, in fact, far truer today in ***2025*** than they might have been in ***1944***:

Unfortunately, I am not in sympathy with the deep hatred that political parties bear today to each other. Politics are just on the surface of human affairs. They do not go deep down into the heart of things or into the profundities of our real nature. They have small connection with our relations to the other world or to our being able to secure the grace of the Almighty.

Why should people who hold one political opinion execrate men on the other side to such an extent that whatever their private character may be, however great their usefulness to the public may be in other directions, however exemplary their conduct may be, why should people hold them up to be the enemies of the future of the nation?

All parties, it seems to me, have their place in politics. No one party has the monopoly of truth or of political wisdom. Each party requires the assistance of the others, if only we knew that political wisdom and political truth are to be found in the doctrines of every organised political party. We ought all to regard one another as allies in the task of serving the country. Perhaps the exigencies of the day may throw us even into some rivalry of actual work, and we may be found on opposite sides of the camp, each trying to negative the work of the other. But we need not traduce the character of the great men on the other side.

**** ****

ON TEMPERANCE OF SPEECH

Young men delight in throwing mud at older people. ***I have suffered a great deal myself.*** *I have known other people who have a title to real greatness and to the gratitude of our country suffer undeservedly at the hands of young men. This is a very special feature of democratic politics. It was not the case at a time when politics had not become democratised. It is much more prevalent in America and England, where politicians have established themselves over a good many generations and where at the moment, if you will* *ask my honest opinion, the converse of democracy is far more in evidence than the good it has done or the good it is likely to do for some time.*

More than property, more than the honour of your wives, more than the affairs of litigation which cast off fellow-feeling, more than all these, political differences seem to call forth from our people the vilest language to be applied to one another. It is a thing that I cannot understand, and it is a thing which I wish were eliminated from the education of our boys, if possible, for ever and for ever.

**** ****

ON THE SUPREME IMPORTANCE OF MUTUAL RESPECT

No young man ought to be taught to think that a leader of high reputation, just because he happens to be on the other side, is a vile man to be abused and to be spoken of as one who has to die, or if he will not die, to be destroyed if the good of India has to be served. I think that that man would be the greatest benefactor of his day who could teach the young in our colleges and schools to think that private merit, the beauties of human character, the dignities of human conduct, are to be found in all political parties, and that it is wrong for a young man to narrow his sympathies and his heart.

That, however, is a desire which is not going to be fulfilled in my time.

It is inconceivable that Srinivasa Sastri may have also foreseen then that the same forlorn desire he voiced on **July 19, 1944,** would continue remaining unfulfilled to this day, the **15th of August, 2025.**

**** **** ****

Chapter 14: "Anti-*Sanatanist* Liberal" or "Orthodox Performative *Brahmin*"? - 1

Srinivasa Sastri viewed ***Dharma*** as both personal ethical conduct and societal duty. He linked it closely to moral responsibility, justice, compassion, and wise governance. If there was only one overriding theme that overshadowed all others in his famous thirty **"Lectures on the *Ramayana*"** 1944, it was this commandment and this alone:

"*Rulers must abide by* ***Dharma****—a combination of righteousness, discipline, and self-restrain*t. And he saw "*Rama, as the model king, (who) embodies the vision of dharma—binding his people together in justice and loyalty founded on ethical leadership and personal virtue.*"

Since Sastri, above all else, held the principle of *Dharma* to be supreme, the question naturally arises in the minds of both admirers and detractors, then as it does now:

~ Was he a **Hindu Orthodox Sanatanist** or a **Hindu Liberal Reformist**? And if he was either one of the two, could he also be described or not with that peculiarly pejorative term often reserved for the so-called "***Hindu Sanghi***" viz. a "Performative Brahmin"?

~ Was he a devout *orthodox Brahmin* in religious outlook? Did Sastri ever wear caste marks on his person as Brahmins did? Did he perform *Sandhyavandanam*? Did he perform ancestral Vedic rites of *pitru-shraadham*? After all, Sastri did passionately hero-worship, did he not, his idol and ideal in life, *Sri Rama* of the *Ramayana*, who in fact, as Valmiki wrote, scrupulously performed both the rites of *Sandhyavandam* and *Pitru-Shraadham...*?

**** ****

Sastri was born into an orthodox Brahmin family and was raised in an environment of strict ritual observance and traditional Hindu values. His father was a Vedic scholar and a devout practitioner of ritual, and his early upbringing included deep exposure to the Sanskrit scriptures, epics, and the cultural life of a traditional Brahmin household.

Sastri maintained a strong personal discipline, placing high value on self-control, piety, and moral conduct, and repeatedly expressed reverence for the ideals of *dharma* (righteousness) and the spiritual teachings of the epics like the *Ramayana* and other Vedic scriptures. He was known to have maintained the typical Brahminical customs, which included performing daily rituals and observing caste marks (such as the *pāṇḍu*, *pundram* or *tilaka*) traditionally worn by Brahmins (although exact specific details of his wearing caste marks on his person are not explicitly documented in public sources or archives; however, his orthodox upbringing does imply such observance). And there is enough historical evidence to show that Sastri did practice traditional Hindu rites including *Sandhyāvaṇḍanam* (the daily ritual-worship performed by orthodox Brahmins), as he adhered closely to Vedic and ritualistic norms in his devotional and family life.

Sastri also participated in *pūjā* for the *ārādhana* (yearly remembrance rituals) connected with the passing away of *sanyāsis* in his family lineage, indicating observance of annual ancestral rites in the strict Brahmin tradition. He also performed *pitṛ-śrāddham* (ancestral rites) annually, as noted from accounts of his observance of yearly rituals connected to the worship and remembrance of ancestors (*pūjā* for *ārādhana*), which aligns with the orthodox Brahminical duties.

D.V. Gundappa (DVG), the famous Kannada litterateur, who was Sastri's biographer, narrates a very telling incident which reveals Sastri's reverence for the spiritual value of the Vedic ritual of *Sandhyavandanam.* Sastri expressed to DVG feelings of deep guilt and regret for having been lax in the performance of the *Sandhyavandanam* ritual due to his ill-health.

**** ****

Sastri with his wife and family had once visited the *Ashram* of the **Sri Sringeri Shankaracharya Muttam** to pay obeisance to the pontiff, **Jagadguru PujyaSri Chandrashekhara Bharati.** The *Shankaracharya* was engaged in *Puja* ritual when Sastri arrived there and humbly requested for an audience with the pontiff.

QUOTE: *The Jagadguru consented and went ahead with the pūjā. After the pūjā, the Jagadguru offered "phala-mantrākṣatā" to Sastri and his wife Lakshmamma and blessed the couple. Something interesting happened at this instance. The Jagadguru placed a golden "tāli" (or "mangala sutra") and a handwritten note in Sastri's hand and said: "You should ask your wife to wear this taali."*

Sastri: "We are privileged, thanks to the blessings of the Guru. As per your command, I shall have her wear this in the Śāradā-devī temple tomorrow. She has lost all confidence looking at the illness I am suffering from, and she is constantly worried about my longevity. I'll act as per the Guru's instruction for her mental well-being. I'll also keep the śhloka safe and remember the same. I can't speak much."

They bowed down to the Guru and returned to their lodge. I then asked Sastri:

Me: "What did you intend to say? What was the śhloka that you mentioned?"

*Sastri: **"I have not been performing the sandhyāvandana regularly. It has, in fact, been quite a long time since I stopped performing the sandhyāvandana.** Such being the case, how can I give my word to the Jagadguru that I will regularly chant the śhloka? The śhloka looks really ordinary. Don't we have hundreds of such śhlokas and "stotras" in our tradition? What is so special about it? However, the person adorning the Guru's pedestal has given it to me with great affection. It is our duty to respect it."* **UNQUOTE**

**** ****

So, given the above facts of Sastri's personal faith, would it not be too easy for any present-day social commentator who, let us say, proudly claims that he or she is wedded to '*secular-liberal values*' and '*social justice*', to label Sastri as a "*Performative Brahmin?*"

Who is a "***performative brahmin?***" This term is used in contemporary social critique and cultural studies to describe how certain individuals or groups publicly display, enact, or emphasize the traits, customs, symbols, or mannerisms associated with being a Brahmin (the priestly, scholarly caste in Hindu tradition)—often for social prestige, authority, or belonging, rather than as a matter of authentic personal spiritual practice or lived tradition. This can involve the conscious use of dress (white clothes, forehead marks), speech patterns, Sanskritized language, and participation in traditional rituals—as *social performance.*

In drama, literature, and public events, Brahmins may be depicted (or self-depict) as calm, wise, charitable, scholarly—projecting virtues commonly associated with Brahmin status and elitism... Sometimes, this is done to claim moral or intellectual authority, rather than resulting from deeper engagement with those ideals.

In political or intellectual contexts, *"performative Brahminness"* might mean publicly enacting Brahminical identity to signal legitimacy or belonging among elite circles—sometimes overshadowing more inclusive or pluralistic values. It can also involve gatekeeping or dominance in academic, cultural, or spiritual spaces.

Dalit and Dravidianist self-proclaimed "anti-caste" writers often use *"performative Brahminness"* to criticize token displays of Brahmin identity (in rituals, ceremonies, or discourse) that imply reinforcement of caste privilege, rather than genuine spiritual practice or egalitarian reform. It's seen as part of the *"Brahminical social order"*—upholding status and hierarchy through outward performance.

So, we now know for sure that Sastri in his own time was viewed by many of his colleagues, political peers and even admirers as an *Anglophile-cum-Sanskritic elitist* of high-brow Tamil Brahmin stock. And therefore, it would be hardly surprising if Sastri were today to be branded a "*performative brahmin?*"

**** ****

Objectively speaking however, the term "*performative brahmin*" must surely ill suit Sastri as definitely as the term "*Sanatanist,*" in its present-day sense, would be mischaracterizing him.

"*Sanatanist*" widely used in contemporary India often signifies a strong, public, and actively political identification with *Sanatana Dharma.* It is also in some cases a strong advocacy for ritual orthodoxy as a social or political project. Many a time it is also virulent opposition to reformist or secular currents.

Sastri's personal record in history shows that he favoured none of the above courses of action. The record shows that his approach to *Sanatana Dharma* was very nuanced and sophisticated.

Sastri did not publicly champion orthodox *Sanatanist* causes or use religion as a political weapon. He was influenced by liberal and reformist traditions within Indian society (notably **Gokhale** and **Ranade**), and his public work was characterized by rational inquiry, moderation, and a focus on ethical universals, not ritual exclusivism. Sastri was part of a generation that sought to purify and reinterpret Hindu traditions, seeking to reject only its superstitions but wholly and categorically emphasizing their ethical core principles and tenets.

While personally devout and respectful of Hindu tradition, Sastri never was a militant orthodox Brahmin in the contemporary political sense. He was liberal in his public engagements, stood for social harmony, and did not involve himself with extremist movements opposed to social reform or secularization. Sastri's own Hindu cultural identity blended seamlessly with liberal, secular political goals because he worked very closely with leaders like Gopal Krishna Gokhale and Mahatma Gandhi, both of whose inclusiveness transcended narrow religious identities— and values that Sastri shared with them and upheld steadfastly. Furthermore, Sastri was a founding member of the **Indian Liberal Party**, which favoured constitutional reforms and opposed separatist tendencies and communal divisions.

If Sastri were present today, his values of liberal constitutionalism, pluralism, social justice, and internationalism would very likely place him in opposition or serious critique of some of the "*hard-core*" or "*hawkish*" Hindutva movement. He would have been found advocating for an Indian movement that embraced all its diversities and upheld a constitutional, inclusive democracy.

So, if Sastri were to be alive today, it would really be a moot question whether he would have been gleefully appropriated as mascot or flagship symbol by the small but very powerful influencer-group in the ***left-liberal-secular anti-Sanatanist intelligentsia*** of India, that has sworn eternal enmity with radical *Hindutva.* In other words, the likes of all the enlisted eminent persons below — belonging to varying professions and walks of life — might certainly have been only too keen to apotheosise Rt. Hon'ble Srinivasa Sastri and use him as their figurehead icon.

Legal and Constitutional Luminaries

Fali S. Nariman, Soli Sorabjee, and other senior advocates: These jurists are known for upholding constitutionalism, minority rights, due process, and civil liberties, echoing Sastri's dedication to rule of law and debate over populist mobilization.

Justice Madan Lokur, Justice R. F. Nariman, Justice A. P. Shah: Some retired judges continue to speak out for constitutional values, judicial independence, and reasoned discourse in public life.

Civil Society Leaders/Activists

Prashant Bhushan, Dr. Syeda Hameed, Harsh Mander, Anjali Bhardwaj: Activists working for civil liberties, minority protections, and social justice within the framework of constitutional democracy. They defend dissent, dialogue, and inclusive citizenship—key to Sastri's philosophy.

Nandan Nilekani, Aruna Roy, Yamini Aiyar: Policy thinkers and reformers who emphasize incremental change, institutional strengthening, education, and evidence-based public action, rather than revolutionary upheaval.

Political Figures with Liberal Leanings

Dr. Shashi Tharoor, Jairam Ramesh, P. Chidambaram (Congress Party): They advocate pluralism, civil liberties, and global engagement—in ways that sometimes echo the liberal constitutional tradition. However, their party and the broader landscape often pull in more populist or minoritarian directions.

(late) *Sitaram Yechury, Brinda Karat* (CPI-M): Though left-of-centre, they sometimes defend the constitutional order and rights for the marginalized; however, their ideological framework is more socialist than liberal.

Scholars, Writers, and Public Intellectuals

Pratap Bhanu Mehta, Ramachandra Guha, Madhav Khosla, and Gautam Bhatia: These writers and thinkers robustly defend constitutionalism, pluralism, federalism, and reasoned engagement in public discourse, standing closer to Sastri's world than electoral politicians do.

Gopalakrishna Gandhi, N. Ram, T. M. Krishna (musician–activist): Advocates of social harmony and democratization of culture, with token respect for tradition alongside reform—a spirit reminiscent of Sastri's syncretic outlook.

Institutions

The Indian Liberal Group, Centre for Civil Society, and a campus debate forums and parliamentary research bodies here and there: They promote dialogue, debate, and a non-polarized vision of progress and reform, working in the spirit of liberal civic argumentation.

However, there is no doubt at least in my mind, that no single individual or party fully embodies Sastri's mix of scholarship, statesmanship, nobility of thought, pluralism, and the ideal of genuine constitutionalism.

Not one of the above eminent persons can be said to qualify as genuine inheritors of Sastri's tradition. Indian public life has few *"inheritors"* of Sastri's legacy because the reality is that his nuanced, principled liberalism is of the kind that cannot survive in the harsh and unconducive conditions of civil society today.... nor within the cynical ecosystem of law, academia, journalism and media. Sastri's genre of lofty *Dharmic-Liberal-Humanism* would be no more a dominant force in contemporary Indian party politics than it was in his own time.

While it can be argued that Sastri's principles remain still profoundly relevant today and might earn him a little respect across political lines, the current political environment in India—with its intensity, fragmentation, and ideological battles—would have no choice but to marginalize/sideline a figure of his nuanced, moderate character. He would a "*respected outsider*" rather than a mainstream party leader or influencer.

**** ****

Srinivasa Sastri thus cannot easily be stereotyped as belonging to any of the categories of the Liberal fraternity that we are all familiar with in today's India. He was neither an *Orthodox* nor a *Performative Brahmin* "***Sanatanis***t," and nor was he a shrill ***"anti-***

Sanatanist *Left-Liberal*" with a heart bleeding blue for secular reformation.

Two separate incidents that involved burning social issues of his times that happened in Sastri's life are clear evidence for the above assessment of the man:

A. *Temple Entry law for Dalits into the* **Guruvayurappan Temple in Kerala** and

B. the *Hindu marriage customs* under the **Sarada Act**.

**** **** ****

Chapter 15
"Anti-*Sanatanist* Liberal" or "Orthodox Performative *Brahmin*?" - 2

Even with the benefit of 20:20 historical hindsight that we enjoy today, and as it was in his own time without it, Srinivasa Sastri could never easily be stereotyped. He was unique in that it could not be said with any certainty whether he was outright an *Orthodox* or *Performative Brahmin* "***Sanatanist***" or otherwise a shrill ***"anti-Sanatanist*** *Left-Liberal*" whose heart bled blue for secular reforms to Hinduism.

Two separate incidents in Sastri's life do support the above assessment of the man. In one he seemed to lean towards Brahmin Orthodoxy but, of course, only in the most liberal, catholic and enlightened sense; and in the other incident, he openly played the part of an *anti-Sanatanist* liberal reformer. The two events were:

(A) *Temple Entry law for Dalits into the* **Guruvayurappan Temple in Kerala** (*which was a continuation of the famous1924-25* ***Vaikom Satyagraha*** *movement in Kerala for Untouchables to gain entry and worship inside Temples)*

(B) The **Sarada Act** that related to Hindu customary law relating to woman's rights. (*The* ***Child Marriage Restraint Act, 1929****, passed on 28 September 1929, in the Imperial Legislative Council of India, fixed the minimum age of marriage for girls at 14 years and boys at 18 years. In 1949, after India's independence, it was amended to fix the age of marriage at 15 for girls, and in 1978 at 18 for girls and 21 for boys. It is popularly known as the* ***Sarda Act****, after its sponsor Harbilas Sarda).*

**** ****

GURUVAYUR TEMPLE ENTRY FOR UNTOUCHABLES

The **Guruvayurappan Temple Satyagraha** was a major campaign in Kerala for Dalit temple entry, led by **K. Kelappan** who was supported by leaders like **Mannathu Padmanabhan** and **A. K. Gopalan**

(Communist Party of India). The struggle included a hunger strike, mass mobilization, and a demand for the right of lower caste Hindus (then called "*untouchables*") to enter the temple.

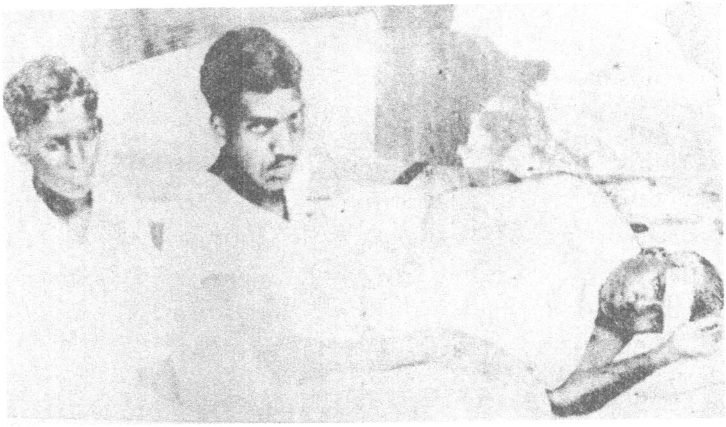

Guruvayurappan Temple Entry Satyagraha

Gandhi took personal interest in the Guruvayurappan agitation. When *K. Kelappan* (imitating Mahatma Gandhi's own political tactics) began a fast-unto-death to press the cause, Gandhi intervened—writing to ask him to break the fast, fearing harm or violence. The *satyagraha* was suspended at Gandhi's request and the issue then gained all-India attention. The *Satyagraha* itself did not immediately succeed in opening the Guruvayurappan temple, but it triggered significant social reform debates. It was only later in **1936,** that the **Temple Entry Proclamation** in Travancore allowed lower castes access to many Kerala temples, marking an important step toward ending ritual exclusion.

Srinivasa Sastri did not play a significant or direct front-line role in the *Guruvayurappan Satyagraha of 1931–32*, though he was aware of the issue and Gandhi, in fact, reached out to him for advice.

YERAVADA CENTRAL PRISON: ***8th November 1932***

Dear Friend and brother,

You will have seen that Guruvayur is being made the centre of attack by the self-styled Sanatanists. Not much time to lose.

I do not know how far your health will let you organise the battle on behalf of the reformers. To the extent it is possible, I would like you to put your great Sanskrit learning at the disposal of the cause.

I am sure you have been thinking of the thing yourself. But I could not restrain myself from sending you a line when I am writing to many friends about the impending storm.

It gives me great joy that I am able to take some work out of the Servants (of India) here.

I do hope you are better.

With love, Yours

M. K. GANDHI

Then on **November 10, 1932,** Gandhiji, referring to Kelappan, issued however a statement urging that the Guruvayurappan *satyagraha* be called off for the time being, but in which he also said that he himself would gladly later join Kelappan!

"I would be in honour bound to fast with him if on or before the first of January next that temple is not opened to the Untouchables, and if it becomes necessary for Sri. Kelappan to resume it."

**** ****

Sending a copy of the above letters he had received from Gandhi to another friend, Sastri wrote:

"In reply I have written two letters (to Gandhi), clearly stating my dissent from his views and my disapproval of his threatened fast. Of course I favour the temple-entry of the untouchables."

And writing to another friend, Sastri also wailed:

"What a predicament I am in! To wish his (Gandhi's) cause success but utterly discountenance his method and his hurry."

Sastri, a staunch constitutionalist and a steadfast moderate, and never an overzealous Hindu reformer, was sympathetic to the cause of temple entry for Dalits. However, he typically advocated negotiation, education, and legal reform rather than direct action or *satyagraha*. Privately, he corresponded about his misgiving to Gandhi:

*"Patience, good-will, and consideration for sincerely held beliefs are essential in matters of faith. Social change, especially concerning places held sacred, comes best through understanding and education, not through pressure— **however righteous the cause**."*

Sastri had pointed out to Gandhi that ancient temples like Guruvayurappan had been administered for centuries strictly in accordance with time and custom honoured Hindu *Agama Sastras* which were the sole authoritative basis of faith upon which temple norms were established and rituals had always been conducted. To interfere with such *Agamas* with the intention to overturn them in a spirit of revolutionary or republican fervour would only do more harm than good to the social fabric of the peoples of India.

Gandhi was obviously receptive to the spirit in which Sastri's two letters to him had been written. And so, referencing Sastri's advice, the Mahatma wrote to a few friends about it:

"Shri Sastri's counsel has always been to avoid any method that would cause bitterness. I have valued his friendships and his faith in the power of reason … His voice carries great moral weight in South India."

Thereafter, once the *Satyagraha* and Kelappan's fast had been called off, Gandhi further wrote to Srinivasa Sastri after having carefully read through both correspondence and all the accompanying material on ***Temple Agama Sastra***s that the latter had made available to him. Gandhi acknowledged the wisdom in Sastri's advice to tread slowly and cautiously on matters related to the faith of the Hindu people in their Temples but refused to accept the overarching authority of the ***Agama Sastras.***

YERAVADA CENTRAL PRISON: ***24th November 1932***

Dear Brother

I had your precious letters. Your criticism soothes. Your silence makes me nervous. Time only deepens my love for you.

Our differences appear to me to be superficial. Deep down I feel and touch the meeting ground, and that is precious.

I do wish I never spoke of God or the Inner Voice or Conscience. But, like Raamnam, however much it may be abused, it has got to be repeated when it is relevant and almost becomes imperative. Truth will receive a deep cut if, for fear of being misunderstood or even being called a fraud, I did not say boldly what I felt to be true.

I carefully read the typed notes you sent me. The reasoning failed to make any appeal to me. The implications of the **Agamas** *are stretched too far by the writer.*

I hope you are keeping well.

With love, Yours

M.K. GANDHI

**** ****

Eighty-five long odd years (!) have passed after the above Sastri-Gandhi correspondence took place. But it is sad irony that even to this day the Hindus of India continue find themselves deeply embroiled and entangled in scores of seemingly irreconcilable and rancorous legal battles in the State High Courts and in the Supreme Court of India too over what limits are there and to what permissible extent, exactly, they must be set to restrain the Constitutional powers a Democratic, Secular Government can invoke and exercise in its interference into religious affairs of Hindu temples by even overturning ancient *Agama Sastras.*

Truly, Srinivasa Sastri -- the oxymoronic *orthodox liberal-hearted Brahmin* from Mylapore -- had possessed such remarkable foresight and wisdom that he did not have to shirk from counselling even the tallest, most dominant political leader in the country of that time, the great Mahatma Gandhi. Sastri did not mince words in warning him that rabble-rousing and rallying Hindu Reformists and Secularists with clarion calls of *Satyagraha, Ahimsa* and *fasts-unto-death,* all would only foment unwarranted revolution inside the ancient temples of India. Such revolutions would only divide the nation, never unite it.

**** **** ****

Chapter 16
"Anti-*Sanatana's* Liberal" or "Orthodox Performative *Brahmin?*" - 3

"THE SARADA ACT 1929"

Sastri deeply respected the *śāstra*-s and Hindu traditions but at the same time he also insisted that tradition must be intelligently interpreted in the light of contemporary science and modern needs. In taking this stand, the Mylaporean *Brahmin-liberal-humanist* clearly stood on the side of the *"anti-Sanatanist Hindu Reformers"* of his times ... and yes, those perhaps of the present day, too, who are in the forefront as champions of Women's Rights amongst several other so-called "*neo-liberal"* causes.

D.V. Gundappa (***DVG***), Sastri's biographer remembered Sastri's philosophical approach to the Hindu *Sastras*, classed under the overarching civilisational umbrella called *Sanatana Dharma*, as being singular. In a talk at the **Kannada Sahitya Parishat, Bangalore**, Sastri had said, DVG wrote, that many scholars merely parroted old texts without adapting doctrines to the present context. The world was changing, Sastri averred, with new knowledge, and *dharma* must evolve accordingly:

"*The traditional scholars must keep in mind the current circumstances and the needs of the time...the perspective of man has been changing, and such changes are neither artificial nor do they go against* **Sathya** *and* **dharma**."

Sastri explained **Sanātana Dharma** as being manifold ways people can approach the Divine and emphasized individual spiritual growth and the pursuit of truth:

"*The essence of Indian religion is to aim at growing and living so that we can grow out of ignorance which veils self-knowledge from our life and become aware of the Divinity within us.*"

Sastri also stood for a Hinduism that was inclusive and universal, rejecting sectarianism or narrow religious identity. He saw Hinduism as a living tradition interacting with other faiths and modern ideals, not rigid dogma:

> "*The Hindu civilization, rooted in Sanātana Dharma, has constantly been enriched by* ***brahma*** *and safeguarded by* ***kṣāttra***."

**** ****

The way Sastri has defined *Sanatana Dharma* above is not just interesting ... it is quite extraordinary indeed!

Sastri invoked two very significant Sanskrit terms: "*brahma*" and "*kshaattra*" which to the Hindu mind should immediately evoke the idea of "***vita contemplativa***" and ***"vita activa"*** which, *prima facie*, may be **Aristotelian** terms but then they clearly refer to two of Vedic civilisational and cultural aspirations of India's most ancient history.

"Vita contemplativa" means the "*contemplative way of life.*" It is the life focused on contemplation, meditation, and intellectual or spiritual reflection. It aims at an inner, spiritual perfection and union with the divine or ultimate truth. This typically is the way of true ***"brahmanic*** living" – but shorn of all casteist connotations.

"Vita activa" means the "*active way of life.*" This path centres on active engagement in the world through moral virtues, social and economic duties, military work, and practical actions. It involves the exercise of honour, prudence, justice, fortitude, temperance and addresses the external, secular activities of life such as labour, work, and political/social action for public good. In other words, this is the true ideal of "*kshaattra*" or the "***kshatriya*** way of life" — again with no casteist connotation attached to the word at all.

Sastri's approach to *Sanatana Dharma* was thus both *Spiritual* and *Secular* at the same time. He viewed Hindu religion, tenets, traditions and institutions as being in essence both *brahma* and *kshaatra* representing the harmony of India's spiritual and social needs.

It was precisely this enlightened approach to Hindu orthodox religious traditions that convinced Srinivasa Sastri that in matters where **Reform** was possible, reasonable and imperative – for the betterment of Hindu society at large -- *Change* should not be anathema to him.

Pujyashree HH Sri Chandrasekhara Bharathi, Sringeri Shankaracharya Muttam (1892–1954 CE)

It was Sastri's conviction about such *Change* which made him a defender of the **Sarada Act**, a legislation which he had no doubt would bring not only justice but also great dignity to the status of all Hindu women in India. In the defence of the *Sarada Act*, which went, some people said, against the grain of Hindu *Sastra and law*, and had angered if not outraged Hindu religious and traditional Brahmin pontiffs such as the **Shankaracharya of Sri Sringeri Mutt**, Srinivasa Sastri was willing and ready to take on the formidable orthodoxy. But he went about doing so --- as is obvious from the narratives below --- in his typically "*inoffensive*," low-key, diplomatic, scholarly and most persuasive way.

**** ****

In the matter of Women's Rights and social dignity for women, it is quite evident that Sastri's convictions were deeply influenced by the *Valmiki Ramayana's* portrayal of the agony and humiliations that Sita had to undergo --- in the heart-rending episodes in the *Yuddha Kandam* and *Uttara Kandam* wherein Rama is seen making it his *Dharmic* duty to demand proof from her of innocence of chastity. Equally, it can be inferred that the same convictions also stemmed from his taste and appreciation of Western literature.

Sastri loved reading the fictional works of English writers like **Thomas Hardy.** One novel was his favourite because in it he found moral grounding for his own views and position on *Women's Rights.* In an essay he wrote as appreciation of Hardy's novel, one can sense from where the empathetic and emphatic support Sastri gave to *Sarada Act* might have found its mainspring.

QUOTE:

"Tess of the D'Urbervilles" *gave a vision, as bright as it was clear, of a problem that had long been vexing me, and for the first time in my experience, set the position of women in correct perspective.*

Hardy, I have no doubt, meant to startle a convention-ridden and heartless world to a consciousness of the essence of chastity by his sub-title "The Story of a Pure Woman." It is audacious, but he makes it out to be just and proper.

The taint is inflicted on Tess while she is hardly aware of what is happening and, the sinister consequence following, she has to pay the severest penalty that is exacted of her sex. Society is no doubt heartless in such cases, but Hardy makes society almost fiendish in its persecution of poor Tess. The victim of a cruel wrong, her subsequent life of high purpose and good deeds does not avail her, and at the end disaster, black and utter disaster, overtakes her until it seems to the reader that Tragedy herself must be horrified.

Our (own) Ahalya, who is in a way suggested to our thoughts by the story of Tess, escapes lightly in comparison, though her sin was committed consciously for the rapture of it. If we reduced the Ramayana scale to human proportions, her penance cleansed her soon enough, and it needed only Rama's touch to restore the unsullied charm, that Brahma had given her at birth.

Hindu society has treated her with divine indulgence. She is placed first among the five good women whose names have only to be remembered once a day to rid us of our grossest sins. Only one of these, Mandodari has a perfectly white record. Sita had a whisper against her, however unjust. Draupadi had more husbands than one. The last one Tara, if she is the wife of Brihaspati, was unfaithful; if she is the Ramayana heroine, (she) changed her husband three times. To say the least, this is a perplexing galaxy of good women.

Yet I am persuaded that it is indicative of a highly tolerant and understanding attitude towards woman, which dates back to a very early period in our story.

How time and custom have hardened our hearts today! We have forgotten the natural standards of the early time and become the slaves of false ideas utterly inconsistent with our nature as human beings. The springs of character would be purified, conduct would be regulated justly, and life would be happy all round, if the relations between men and women could be based on mutual forbearance and understanding as in olden times and forgiveness and tolerance were regarded as excellences not only in wives but equally in husbands.

UNQUOTE

In Sastri's own mind thus, the enactment of the *Sarada Act* was a way in which Hindu society could go back to its past when Indian womanhood was treated "*with divine indulgence*" ... so that Indian women received the dignity that was their birthright, and all got once again *"placed first among the five good women whose names have only to be remembered once a day to rid us of our grossest sins."*

It was precisely with that spirit within him that he and the *Pontiff of Sri Sringeri Muttam*, **Pujyasri Chandrasekhara Bharathi** engaged in a scholarly debate over whether the *Sarada Act* was or was not a violation of Hindu *Dharma Sastras*.

D.V. Gundappa (DVG) in his biography of Sastri gave an enthralling eye-witness account of that vigorous but graceful debate between a presiding *yogi* and an erstwhile *commissar*.

**** ****

QUOTE:

Sri Chandrashekhar Bharati was the presiding *Jagadguru* during our visit to **Sringeri** back then. About a couple of weeks before Sastri's visit to Sringeri, the *Jagadguru* had taken up a certain oath – he had stopped delivering lectures and giving lessons. All the resident students and scholars had been instructed to constantly chant the *Gāyatrī-mantra* on those days. The reason for this will be clear in the due course of my writing. Srinivasa Sastri who was visiting Sringeri with his family had the *darśan* ('a meeting/ an audience with a deity/ Guru') of the *Svāmi* during the *pūjā*, as it was premediated. The *Svāmi* enquired about his well-being and instructed Sastri in the following manner:

"I am glad that you have come here. It seems like Śāradā-devī (the presiding deity of Sringeri) herself has brought you here – to get her task executed. It is something important in the view of safeguarding our dharma. I have heard that there is a certain law pertaining to the Hindu marriages that is being discussed at the parliament in Delhi. Apparently, it is called the ***'Sharada Bill'****. What kind of times are these?* ***Should we name an idea that is totally contrary to Śāradā-devī's view after her?*** *We certainly need to do something about this strange set of circumstances. The emperor has honoured you by including you in his* ***Privy Council****. I have heard that the members of the council can meet the Viceroy in person and can explain their views to him. You should meet the Viceroy and appropriately advise him such that this* ***Apasmārāsura*** *(a demon) is stopped immediately. We (royal 'we') have given up all teaching and lectures for the last fifteen days with the hope of countering the attempts being made by the Bill at the Centre. We have instructed all the students and scholars residing here to constantly chant the "Gāyatrī-mantra". We have taken up an oath to go ahead with this lifestyle until our prayer is answered".*

Sastri, who heard this brief speech of the Jagadguru replied:

"It is time for the pūjā now. We will need time to think out the matter that you have just touched upon. If you could please permit me to do so, let us discuss this matter on another occasion".

The following day, we spoke about the wedding rituals at the mutt. The conversation between the *Jagadguru* and Srinivasa Sastri was in Tamil – - Tamil mixed with Sanskrit – I am sure that the readers would have guessed this. Sastri put forth the matter in *two dimensions* – one *personal* and the other related to the *śāstra*. He said –

"The Bill says that the minimum age for the marriage of girls needs to be increased. I too have always had the same opinion. A few years back when I was a member of the Legislative Council of Madras, I had felt that this was a welcome change. I had even drafted my thoughts and brought it before the council for discussion. Back then, the council was full of government officials, and it was also a pre-decided norm that the governing council would not interfere in the religious matters. Thus, my suggestion was not taken up for serious discussion. My opinion, however, has still remained the same. Somebody else has put forward the same idea at the Centre and is it right for me to oppose it? When somebody else is supporting the idea that I have always had, how can

I oppose it? Moreover, in about three to four weddings that have taken place in my own family, the bride was much older than the recommended age. It is not merely my opinion but what I have been practising too. The two together can be helpful in bringing the required change in the system. Therefore, it does not seem right for me to oppose the Sharada Bill".

"*Let me now move on to the second aspect connected with the issue.*

From what I gather from the śāstras, it is only after a girl attains her puberty and her menstrual cycles start, she should be given in marriage. I have gone through quite a number of works on this subject and have carried out some research. We don't find any evidence in the śruti and the smṛtis for the practise of getting a young girl married, as is in vogue today. Most people in our country today get a girl who is between eight and ten years old married. We will need to understand that this practise is not very ancient and has come into vogue due to some historical reasons. We can only guess that people gave up the ancient tradition and took to getting girls married in their childhood ***(bālya-vivāha)*** *because of some historical developments.*

*We should examine the mantras that are used as a part of the vivāha (wedding) ceremony. There is a mantra that goes '**ārohūraṃ** ...'. The meaning in this and other mantras is very clear. This is not something you would tell a girl who is eight or ten years old. The meaning of the mantra goes well only with a matured girl. Let us also contemplate upon the procedure of conducting a wedding. We know that the married couple will need to spend three nights sharing the bed. After this, as per the **sūtra – 'tṛtīyāyāmapararātrau'**, the husband will need to perform the **visarjana** of **viśvāvasu** and **gandharvas.** This is to be followed by the **Caturthi-karma**. What does this mean? It only means that the girl is ready to take part in the marital life. We can infer this from a close examination of the **gṛhya-sūtras*** (Vedic *dharma sastra* pertaining to household rites)

Sringeri Svāmī: I have not gone through the *gṛhya-sūtras*...

Sastri: The ***gṛhya-sūtras*** are not relevant for the ***yati-āśrama***, i.e., for *sanyāsis*. However, the matter under discussion relates to the ***gṛhastha-dharma***. I feel that we will need to take ***gṛhya-sūtras*** as our guidebook in these matters.

Sringeri Svāmī: *Ahaa!* That is right indeed... I shall examine the ***gṛhya-sūtras*** and then arrive at a conclusion on this matter.

UNQUOTE

**** ****

The forceful but un-polemical way in which Sastri put forward his "*reformist*" views to the Pontiff of the Sringeri Mutt on the issue of Hindu Child-Marriage custom was anything but argumentative. It was substantive and couched in polite words that the *Jagadguru* himself could easily appreciate from the standpoint of his high level as a great authority himself on many Hindu scriptural texts.

Sastri was careful not to strike any posture of passionate zeal or self-righteous rhetoric that a lesser *Hindu Reformer* of his time might have adopted under the circumstances. Instead, Sastri's low-key, measured representation to the Pontiff stuck simply to cool logic and to a dispassionate interpretation of the Hindu *Dharma sastras.*

Going by the account of the meeting as given by DVG, we may conclude that the *Sringeri Jagadguru Shankaracharya* did, of course, seem to have immediately understood and graciously appreciated Sastri's averments. But then for the sake of our own understanding of all the scholarly allusions Sastri had made for his case i.e. references to the relevant "***vivaaha***" ritual mantras, it would be worth our while to acquaint ourselves, even if only very sketchily, about what the Hindu ***"gruhya sutras***" state in the matter.

**** ****

a. The *"ārohūraṃ"* mantra refers to the *Asmarohanam* (the *Ritual of Ascending the Grinding Stone*) during the Vedic marriage ceremony. This ritual symbolizes the bride's strength, steadfastness, and her resolve for marital duties. *"Ascend the stone. Like this stone, be firm, resolute, and strong in your household responsibilities and duties."*

As the bride places her foot on the *grinding stone,* she is blessed to emulate the unyielding and stable nature of the stone—signifying her strength of character, fortitude in family life, and ability to withstand challenges.

आरोहणं शिलाया: स्थिरा भव सखाय सधूत्वम अनुशा

"ārohāṇāṃ śilāyāḥ asmasā tvam sthirā bhava śilāyāḥ ārohaṇāṃ"....
chanted with the following Rig Veda mantra:

तिष्ठा शिलायाम् अन्वेति त्वं
स्थिरा भव गार्हपत्येषु

b. The *sutra* phrase **'tṛtīyāyāmapararātrau'** refers to the *third night of the marriage ceremony* after the wedding day. In this context, the groom is said to perform ***visarjana*** (i.e. "sending off" or "dismissing") of the *viśvāvasus* and the *gandharvas* and is then followed by the ***Caturthi-karma*** (i.e. the "fourth" ritual act).

- *Viśvāvasu* and *Gandharvas* are celestial beings often associated with divine attendants, guardians, or spirits connected to natural forces, marriage, and music in Vedic literature. In the marriage context, the bride is traditionally believed to be attended by these benevolent spirits or guardians during certain rites.

- Performing *visarjana* of these celestial spirits or beings signifies formally releasing them or dismissing their protective presence around the bride. Such "dismissal" signifies the marking of her transition from girlhood to married womanhood, emphasizing that her guardianship by the celestial beings now comes to an end and henceforth it is the groom and the new husband's family that shall protect the bride.

- This ritual symbolizes the bride's complete acceptance into the groom's family and her severance from previous under protective supernatural guardians. It also marks the bride's readiness to fully assume new familial and social responsibilities. It purifies and completes the linking of the couple according to cosmic and spiritual order in line with Vedic traditions.

- After the *visarjana* of these celestial attendants, the ***Chaturthi-karma*** is performed. This fourth ritual action often relates to specific rites that stabilize the marriage bond, invoke blessings on the couple, and ensure household prosperity. The exact procedures of *Caturthi-karma* vary by Vedic tradition but include fire-offerings, recitations of sacred mantras, and ritual offerings that sanctify the union and household.

Overall, these rites reflect the deep spiritual and cosmic dimensions of the Vedic marriage, emphasizing transformation, protection, and sanctity of the marital relationship beyond the social contract.

Sastri's sound reasoning therefore was that all the rituals described above — being reflective of deep, spiritual and the cosmic dimensions of the Vedic marriage sacrament, which was indeed more than a mere *social contract*, could not really have been formulated by the *Dharma sastra* or the *"gruhya-sutras"* keeping in mind a mere, pre-pubic, innocent and uncomprehending little girl-bride in mind.

**** ****

In the above encounter with the **Pujyashree Sringeri Mutt Sri Jagadguru Shankaracharya**, Srinivasa Sastry's credentials as both a "*Sanatanist-Liberal*" (no matter how oxymoronic the term may sound!) as well as an "*Orthodox Performative Brahmin*" were conclusively established.

**** **** ****

Chapter 17
A streak of "*rashtravadi*"?

Srinivasa Sastri, in so far as we have studied him in the foregoing pages, was a man who never could be stereotyped as either *this or that* type of votary of any particular political ideology or as anyone who could be easily swayed by any extreme notions of *Nationalism*, *Patriotism* or *Liberalism*. And nor was he any inveterate Hindu *Sanatanist*, *Anti-Sanatana Secularist* .... nor any mere *Performative Orthodox Brahmin*... Sastri never did fit neatly into any pigeon-hole. As many of his vast circle of political colleagues found to their consternation, in the then prevailing political discourse of India and Great Britain, Sastri often seemed a square peg in a round hole.

The question however may be asked:

Judging by how present-day yardsticks are applied to know what is a man's core political affiliation, could it be said that there was a certain furtive streak in Srinivasa Sastri's that suggested that he might have been a ***Hindutva-vaadin*** ... i.e. a nationalist who teetered almost on the border of jingoistic '*raashtra-vaada*'?

A pointed question as above, however, would naturally raise a few corollaries such as the following:

- Do Sastri's professed and practised values of liberalism have any resemblance to those of today's so-called "*Liberals*" in India or to the so-called grander notions of "*neo-liberalism*" in the Western world?
- If Sastri had been alive today, would he have made common cause with those Indian politicians today calling themselves champions of liberal values.... and of the so-called "**soul of India**"?
- If Sastri were to be living today amongst which side of the "*Hindutva-vaada*" debate, would he have veered towards?

In a very moving condolence message that she sent to the family of Sastri on his demise, the poetess-patriot, **Sarojini Naidu**, wrote these famous lines which provide the glimmer of a clue that leads to answers for the questions above. She said:

"He (Sastri) wrote to me long ago (that) "I have lived too long in the shelter of the schoolroom to be able to adjust myself to the noise of the marketplace". But, although his approach to political problems was somewhat cautious and even conservative, in recent years he seemed to have developed closer sympathy with the more dynamic ideals and programmes of the ***more actively nationalist sections of the Indian people."***

There was no doubt that between 1942 and 1946 when he died, Srinivasa Sastri's innate "*cautious conservatism*" of spirit and mentality came under severe stress and he found himself on occasions, rare though, when he found himself involuntarily developing, as Sarojini Naidu accurately put it, a "*closer sympathy with the more dynamic ideals and programmes of the more actively-nationalist sections of the Indian people."* Only in that limited sense in which the poetess characterised him could it be said that Sastri also tended to lean a bit towards "*Hindutva-vaada*".

**** ****

In January 1943, C. Rajagopalachari (Rajaji) had mooted the idea of conceding Pakistan and his canvassing for it began increasing. Although some in the *Indian National Congress Party* were reluctant to openly endorse the Rajaji's proposal, support for it from even non-Congress leaders was seen to be muted but not cold.

In January 1943, the **Council of the Servants of India Society**, of which Sastri was a long-standing and eminent member, by a majority vote, lent secret support to the partition of India. The Society directed its members to refrain from opposing Rajaji's idea which it was well known had Gandhi's blessings and Nehru's backing. When the Society's decision and the directive were conveyed to Sastri, who was firmly and fundamentally opposed to the idea of Partition, he felt so shocked and distressed that he forthwith submitted his resignation from the Society.

In his letter of February 27, 1943, to a colleague in the Society, Sastri said:

"I am conscious I am no longer useful or a source of strength to the Society. Age and conformity to old ways of thought make me a relic of a former age! It is as much as I can expect to be tolerated as an object of interest. Time has run rapidly, while I stand still. I realise that I must not become a positive obstruction."

Three months later -- during which period while his resignation letter remained unacknowledged by the Society -- the Society's governing body had a rethink on the issue and advised its members of its revised stand on the matter viz.: the Society does not oppose the idea officially but its members are free to express their individual opposition to the idea of Partition and Pakistan.

"I understand (from Chimanlal Setalvad, a jurist and barrister in Bombay), that the President has restored the status quo and allowed members to speak and write against Pakistan if they are so minded. If this be the case, I need not press my application for release. My sense of relief is almost a positive happiness. A tie of thirty-five years, dear to me as life itself, to which I owe all I care for and with which I am identified in the eyes of the world, is not to be snapped. Be sure I am to the Society the same as ever."

Sastri thus withdrew his resignation from the Society but a gnawing sense of unease he felt now over the looming prospect of the political vivisection of India by the British Government and, moreover, the *Indian National Congress* under Gandhi and Nehru acquiescing with it too via Rajaji's proposal, began deeply rankling and disturbing his mind. And that was when Sastri's latent Hindu nationalistic instincts or sentiments got aroused. He just could not digest the idea of India being partitioned to appease the Muslim population and Mohammed Ali Jinnah.

In a passionately worded private letter to Gandhi, Sastri gave voice to his own hurt **"national pride."** The words were adulatory of Gandhi, but the message was clearly meant to chide. Gandhi was "hero-worshipped" as a "saint" who, Sastri said, "experimented with truth and courage." The letter was adulatory, yes, but it is difficult to read it today and not miss the veiled sarcasm in the tone of Sastri's every phrase and line:

"I judge you as a saint who has the gift of seeing the truth and courage to experiment with it -- and in the experiment has had more success than most saints so called.

That is why I rejoiced in your enunciation and proclamation of the non-violence doctrine, unadulterated and pure, though the Philistine world jeered. Nor can you put me off by an outburst of your humility and confession of inconsistency, weakness, corruption of the soul and so on. This only exalts you the more in my hero-worshipping mind, making your merits the more lustrous and your blemishes, alas, the more glowing.

I place you along with the philosophers and ethicists of fame. The pursuit of abstract thought and the practice of austerities belong to us in India by heredity. To see you descend on occasions from the heights, I feel bereft of my natural garment, disrobed of my national pride."

Earlier, in April 1944, the Mahatma had himself revealed that he had agreed to the principle of the partition of India when Rajagopalachari pressed it on him in 1943. Accordingly, on September 24, 1944, he informed Mohammed Ali Jinnah the leader of the Indian Muslim League that was demanding a separate Pakistan, that he would commend Partition, but under certain conditions. Jinnah rejected those conditions outright. Wavell, and even Amery (the British Secretary of State for India in London), felt that the British Government should initiate some steps for Partition and no longer wait on any preliminary communal agreement between the two Indian leaders.

**** ****

In his well-researched biography of Srinivasa Sastri, ***Kodanda Rao,*** narrates:

QUOTE:

The news that the Mahatma had agreed to *Partition*, if only in principle and subject to conditions, created a terrific controversy. The *Nationalists* were in two minds; they were dead against Partition but at the same time they saw no hope of political advance without it. An increasing number of them felt obliged to concede Pakistan but shrank from (openly) avowing it and took up an attitude of ambiguous neutrality.

Sastri was profoundly disappointed with the Mahatma and for the first time used a strong expression of disapproval in a personal letter of **August 11, 1944,** to a colleague.

"Gandhi has sold us. He hates the British Raj so much so would use any means of ending it. Hates, of course, is my word. G. (Gandhi-ji) will call it by some other name."

Sastri also wrote to the Mahatma and some others that he was ***"boiling over and should burst out."***

UNQUOTE

The bitter controversy over the issue of Pakistan and the increasingly frequent talk of "*civil war*" created alarm in every one's, including Sastri's, minds.

It was at that time that the *Tej Bahadur Sapru* (1875-1949, another freedom fighter who had left the INC to found the *Liberal Party of India*) who was a leading member of the **Hindu Mahasabha**, and a close associate of Sastri, proposed a conference of non-Congress Party leaders to find a way out. Sastri was invited to accept the Presidentship of it.

Sastri declined. In his letter of **August 25, 1944**, to a colleague, he explained his reasons:

"I never had any fight in me. Now I am useless for a warm debate. The other day I suffered during and after a speech so much that I resolved never to go on a platform again. Yesterday, however, I spoke on the same subject for a trifle of a hundred minutes! Repentance holds me at the moment, but I shan't take an oath."

In another letter of **September 1, 1944,** to his colleague, Sastri referred to the conversation he had with Rajagopalachari about Congress Party's "*repentance*" and, at the same time, the Mahatma's offer to accept Muslim rule! And it was in that very same letter, for perhaps the very first time in his life, that Sastri thought it fit not to conceal what Sarojini Naidu later was able to discern to be his growing "*sympathy with the more dynamic ideals and programmes of the more actively nationalist sections of the Indian people.*"

Sastri referred to the conversation he had with Rajagopalachari by quoting the hard-core *Hindutva-vaadi*, militant freedom-fighter and the leader of the *Hindu Mahasabha*, **Veer Damodar Savarkar**:

*"Have you seen a typewritten statement over **Savarkar's** signature? In it he says several things. Two of these are:*

The Congress people, now free, recently celebrated a "Repentance Day!"

Gandhi, while in the Aga Khan Palace, sent the Viceroy a letter suggesting that the British Power be transferred to the Muslim League and Jinnah be given a free hand and Gandhi would persuade Congress to accept the Muslim line.

*"Both are true, though Savarkar has twisted the text somewhat. On the sands of the (Marina) beach here, Madras, one evening I asked C.R (**Rajaji**), who comes there almost daily, whether the letter was true. He confirmed the substance and proceeded to defend it. **I lost my temper and, raising my voice, exclaimed that I wholly repudiated it and that it was damned surrender. I got ill and suffered most of the night.***

*"I believe there are more of those **against** than there are **for** Pakistan. Still here, in Madras at all events, the **antis** won't come out and give battle, while the other chaps are very vocal. Why is this? A hush has fallen on people, as though a natural phenomenon of terrific power was in progress, and we can only wait for it to do its worst and come to an end. **I am feeble, though all afire and daren't get excited**."*

From the correspondence above, it is clear that on the matter of Partition of India for the sake of appeasing the Muslims with a separate Pakistan, Srinivasa Sastri openly found himself with the "*more actively nationalist sections of the Indian people*," namely the "*Savarkarites*" of those times and of those who in the present day are often branded as rabid *"Hindutva-vaadis."*

**** ****

That Sastri --- as he himself had admitted in writing, -- was simply ***"boiling over"*** the fact which he himself had earlier described in damning words viz.: ***"Gandhi has sold us"....*** and that he felt he ***"should burst out,"*** clearly reveals the state of his distressed mind at that point of time in history. Also, he was a man devastated by the fast-paced political developments he was witnessing then all around him, all orchestrated and managed by the *Indian National Congress* under the leadership of Nehru and Rajaji and by the Indian Muslim League under Jinnah ... and all which filled Sastri with grim foreboding that they were inevitably leading to a historic disaster in the making -- **the Partition of India**.

The biographer *Kodanda Rao* writes:

QUOTE

Nevertheless, Sastri (from his home in Mylapore in Madras) kept up a pretty sustained and wholly uncompromising crusade against the partition of India.

On ***October 24, 1945,*** *just about six months before his death, he along with three other Indian Nationalists, issued a statement on the subject.*

"We think it our duty, and the duty of all who share our views, to give expression to our concern and raise a timely warning as to the direction in which we are drifting. None of us is clear as to the precise implications of the ***two-nation theory.***

Much less perhaps are those who advocate it. The country has never been given any precise details of the territorial division of the country and the lines of demarcation between the two Indias. When Mr. Jinnah is asked to define the territorial demarcation, he has always evaded the issue by demanding that, in the first instance, the claim of the two-nation theory should be granted as the basis of any further negotiations. Those of us, therefore, who are definitely opposed to the very idea of breaking up the unity of India suffer under a handicap as we are not in a position to know precisely the nature of Mr. Jinnah's Pakistan."

The statement strongly criticised the Mahatma and the Congress for their surrender to the Muslim League.

"No measure and no rapprochement could have been so fatal to the unity of India as the Congress Resolution bearing on the right of self-determination for the federating units and the even more regrettable negotiations which took place a year ago between Mr. Gandhi and the spokesman of the Muslim League."

**** ****

It was thus truly a sad, cruelly ironic turn of events in the life of the Rt. Hon'ble Srinivasa Sastri that a moment descended so suddenly and so unexpectedly in his illustrious career as freedom fighter for India when he found himself, an uncompromising *Liberal-Humanist* of the finest order, being forced by overpowering historical circumstances to have to speak the same sort of language as today's *Hindutva-vaadins....*

**** **** ****

Chapter 18: New Delhi ignores, Durban short shrifts and Mylapore forgets him

In the last ten years, **Prime Minister's Narendra Modi's** has made more than one high-profile State visit to South Africa. His public addresses there in Durban focused primarily on Mahatma Gandhi, with ceremonial visits, of course, made to places like Durban associated with Gandhi's life and message. There are extensive media coverage and official documentation of these tributes.

Significantly, other eminent Indian persons too with direct South African connection like **Ela Gandhi** and events relating to Gandhian movements and to the **Sastri College** (*founded by Srinivasa Sastri*) have been honoured and recognized locally in South Africa, with alumni gatherings and celebrations acknowledging Sastri's lasting contributions to Indian education and upliftment there. However, there is no evidence in government press releases, major news coverage, or public speeches of Sri. Narendra Modi directly mentioning or honouring Srinivasa Sastri on these visits—despite Sastri's foundational role as **India's first agent to South Africa** and his lasting educational legacy. In the last decade, local communities in South Africa nonetheless continue to respect Sastri's legacy in the sphere of Education.

While previous Prime Ministers of India and their governments may have had various priorities for visits abroad, from a historical and diplomatic standpoint, not acknowledging Srinivasa Sastri's role is a significant lapse on the part of Narendra Modi and predecessors—and one that ought to be meaningfully addressed in future commemorations or cultural exchanges. Such recognition would enrich the narrative of India-South Africa relations and serve as a reminder of the many individuals like Sastri who worked for justice, dignity, and friendship between the two nations.

**** ****

India's Home Minister, Amit Shah, recently made a public statement declaring that ***"soon, in India, English speakers would feel ashamed,"*** arguing that the dominance of English represents *elite privilege* and *cultural detachment from the broader Indian society.*

Shah's remarks were made during some author's book-launch event in New Delhi. The media reported his comments and were widely interpreted as a critique of English as an *elitist language* and as part of the ongoing effort to centre Indian languages in public life. Shah then went on to emphasize that *"the languages of our country are the ornament of our culture,"* and asserted, *"Without them, we would not have been Bharatiya. Our history, our culture, our Dharma – these cannot be understood in foreign languages."* Shah's statement was seen as a call to efface the perceived ***elitism of English*** from India and to shift cultural and institutional focus toward Indian languages.

In voicing such blatant disdain for the English language, calling it an elitist tongue that eventually Indian languages must banish from India, Amit Shah was articulating an extreme Hindu Right Wing or *Hindutva* aspiration common to mass-populations in the vast *Hindi-Belt* of North India.

What Amit Shah obviously did not know was that love of English *more* did not necessarily mean love of Indian languages *less.*

Srinivasa Sastri was the best example of such ardent lovers of both English as well as ancient Sanskrit which was the root language of ancient India -- in fact, the mother of all other Indian languages of the present -- but which many people believed was no less an *"elitist" language.*

Sri. Amit Shah's vehement statement revealed a strange *Hindutva* paradox:

On the one hand, it was a pronouncement of a Hindutva agenda that means to revive, and resurrect from the dead, *elitist Sanskrit;* and on the other hand, there was also this wish for so-called "*elitist English*", that was still alive and thriving, to be banished from India or dead. It was Sastri however who had brought home to millions of Indians who knew no Sanskrit at all, all the sublimity of *Valmiki's Ramayana*, enabling them thus to overcome the language handicap and still be able to creatively appreciate the epic through the medium of English.

One today wonders how Sastri might have responded to Amit Shah calling him an unabashed *Anglophile* or to Shah's tirade against the English language. Perhaps in typically *"inoffensive"* manner, he would have reminded our powerful Home Minister that it was mastery of the English language that had enabled Sastri to contribute to the Indian freedom struggle in ways for which even Mahatma Gandhi had expressed not only admiration and appreciation but also gratitude.

It was the English language, polished oratory, and constitutional approach that had made Sastri, yes, ***an elite*** diplomat into a consummate international representative of Indian interests. It had enabled him to successfully engage with British political leaders and at global forums like the *League of Nations, the Imperial and diplomatic missions to South Africa and the UK* and speak with authority on matters like even the creation of the *United Nations Organisation.*

Sastri might also have deigned to give Amit Shah a lesson in history to help him understand how *Anglophile elites* like Sastri had contributed essential diplomatic skills and constitutional knowledge to gain international legitimacy for India's independence struggle; how a pluralistic nationalist movement balancing elite negotiation and mass Gandhian resistance movement was thus created. And why despite such valuable contributions, people like Sastri were still disdained by radical nationalists for their perceived *Anglophilia* and "*elitism.*" It was unfair and uncharitable.

**** ****

The renowned Tamil litterateur, novelist, scholar and *Sahitya Akademie Award* winner, *Indira Parthasarathy* once shared a wry piece of trivia with me in a private message about how in New Delhi, the name of the Rt. Hon'ble Srinivasa Sastri had been completely ignored and erased from public memory:

"In New Delhi many years ago, a new locality that came into existence was named "Srinivasapuri" to honour the memory of Srinivasa Sastri. But subsequently they forgot after which Srinivas exactly the neighbourhood was so named. The common belief among Delhi-ites thereafter became that it was named after Lord Balaji, the Deity of Tirupathi!"

**** ****

New Delhi is the capital city of India. It has served as the crucible and centre in which all post-Independence political churning took place --- of ideas, ideology and notions of all kinds had been brewed there... *Hindu Nationalism and Hindutva, Nehru's conceptions of Socialism and Secularism, the idea of Constitutionalism, Rule of Law, Non-Alignment foreign policy, and the ideas of Civil Rights, Freedom of the press and speech a*nd not to speak of *Indian federalism* and that grand *idea of "unity in diversity"*... and many newer forms of thinking later all mutating and growing therefrom.

In such a dynamic intellectual milieu and ideological cauldron as New Delhi was, Srinivasa Sastri, one would have expected, would have come to be ever remembered fondly, and saluted too, for his cerebral brilliance and such valuable contributions to the country's historic affairs that he had made. What then possibly could be the reasons for a man of such great stature to have been given the short shrift by New Delhi that *Prime Ministers* and *Home Ministers of India,* past and present, hardly remembered or cared to mention him even in passing in their public speeches, either in India or in South Africa, in acknowledgment of his many-faceted accomplishments in life?

**** ****

IN historical hindsight that one possesses today, could it be said that Sastri's stature in the Indian political landscape of his times was something that of a political gadfly? One who everyone respected, of course, but who, often, they saw as a stormy petrel of sorts? Was that why none felt comfortable with him? ... With the sole exception of Mahatma Gandhi, of course.

Sastri was not a political gadfly in the sense of a pestering or provoking irritation; nor was he a hated stormy petrel stirring up revolt. He was genuinely revered for his intellect, moral courage, and tact, often called upon to mediate or articulate the moderate nationalist viewpoint. However, his moderate, liberal stance sometimes did *frustrate radicals*, and his *cautious nature occasionally drew criticism*, but even then, *he was never hated*—his reputation remained sterling across the Indian political landscape.

Yet, it is true that Sastri never belonged nor was he warmly embraced by and accepted into any established organisation!

The complex reality of Srinivasa Sastri's career path was that, everywhere, it was marked by profound respect from all quarters but also with a certain "***outsider***" status tagged to it. He was in many ways a *paradox*. He was *admired* by all, yet he remained *peripheral* to all. The reasons that can be adduced for such a paradox may well be explored along the following lines:

1. *Independence of Mind*: Sastri's unwavering commitment to principle, truth, and constitutionalism made him difficult to fully assimilate into any group or party. He followed his conscience rather than the majority or the mood of the movement—even when this meant walking alone... "*eklo chalo re...!*"

2. *Reluctant Political Affiliations*: He started his career in the *Indian National Congress* but was uncomfortable with its drift toward mass agitation, civil disobedience and Gandhian style *satyagraha*. He left the *Congress* when it conflicted with his convictions, joined the *Servants of India Society* but didn't truly belong there either. And then he helped found the *Indian Liberal Federation*—which, despite initial hope, remained just a marginal parliamentary force.

3. *Leadership Without a Following:* Sastri was never a charismatic mass leader or populist. He was too scholarly, too urbane, and too principled for populist politics. His politics was about reasoned persuasion, not emotion or mobilization.

4. *At odds with the political zeitgeist:* He was sceptical of both revolutionary nationalism and state socialism, which became the dominant idioms in twentieth-century India. Even the *British government* hesitated about him—respecting his intellect and moderation, but wary of his insistence on equality and rights for Indians.

5. *Geographical Limitation*: Outside South India, Sastri's fame did not match that of Gandhi or Nehru, since he was not given to mass movements or popular agitation.

6. *Relationship with National Leaders:* Nehru, Rajaji, and Patel found Sastri a formidable intellect and moral presence but too independent-minded and uncompromising for their coalition-building and power politics. He was admired rather than trusted as a fellow strategist.

- PANDIT ***Jawaharlal Nehru*** in his *Autobiography*, published in ***1936***, was highly critical of Sastri. He had not met Sastri often and long enough to form a close personal friendship which could rise above political differences. When he had freshly returned from England about 1912, he heard a speech of Sastri in Allahabad which gave him a *"great shock,"* because Sastri, according to Nehru, had advised students to obey and be respectful to their teachers and observe the rules and regulations of constituted authorities. The advice seemed to Nehru to be *"goody-goody"* and *"platitudinous"* and *"somewhat undesirable."* Though he admitted that Sastri had not used the "*hard word,*" he formed the impression that Sastri advocated students' *"spying"* on one another and acting as *informers*! He was aghast at such advice and felt that there was a great deal of difference between his morality and Sastri's.

- Sastri refrained from replying to Nehru's criticisms and preferred to put up with them silently. Years later he revealed his reaction, which he called his "*drawback*" in his Tamil autobiography, *"If I Live Again"* (freely translated here):

- *"When one criticises me in the papers or on the platform it is not my practice at once to enter into a controversy and immediately answer the criticism. If any misstatement has been made, I would correct it. For a long time, I suffered greatly on account of this. Some time back, a few years ago, a patriot of unparalleled eminence wrote a book. It sold in lakhs. Few were there who did not read it. In that book he criticised me at great length and subjected me to humiliation. Several friends of mine, feeling that it was unjust criticism, prompted me to reply in defence. To me it appeared unnecessary. Though I had the fear that the younger generation on reading this book would have a very low opinion of me I thought that there was no way out and put up with it. But this idea of mine is by no means the outcome of the Gita doctrine that we must treat praise and blame alike. Nevertheless, I do have an immense faith and desire to live up to that doctrine."* (**Letters of Srinivasa Sastri, *pp. 135-136***).
- In 1940, Sastri in a moment of introspection and self-deprecation made this remark about himself: *"I may make a general confession that I am particularly weak-minded. I cannot come to strong and decided resolutions. I am in the habit of looking round and round; of weighing things in the scales of right and wrong; and, as you know, a man who thinks too much of right and wrong is apt to land himself in utter confusion. For, the moment of action is gone; time for decision is left behind."*

7. A *"Conscience-Keeper," Not Kingmaker:* Sastri's destiny was to be heard and heeded by the influential, but seldom to lead the crowd or control an organization.

Sastri's legacy thus was his personal example which was his own unique one. It was one of rectitude, learning, and statesmanship—an influential *outsider*, respected but rarely embraced, who never did quite *"fit"* anywhere and yet left an indelible imprint on every space he occupied. Sastri's story in that respect is emblematic of the intellectual or moral giant whose devotion to principles places him eternally outside the inner circles of power, but always at the centre of conscience and public respect.

This unique position of Sastri, neither fully *"in"* nor *"out,"* was both his greatness and his solitude.

**** ****

Would Srinivasa Sastri's liberalism qualify as true ***Liberalism*** as we know it to be in the world today?

Sastri's liberalism bears far more resemblance to **"classical liberalism"** or **"liberal constitutionalism"** than to contemporary **neo-liberalism.** His was a philosophy of gradual reform, social justice, and constitutional safeguards, not one of market deregulation or state retrenchment. He stands closer to 19th and early 20th century *political* liberals than to late 20th century *economic* neo-liberals.

Sastri's liberalism was an ***article of faith,*** not just strategy or rhetoric. He valued intellectual honesty and detested political posturing or cynical branding. If modern politicians used *"liberalism"* as a mere label, without substance, he would have called them out.

Sastri at the same time also strongly opposed extra-constitutional protest and civil disobedience except in the most extreme circumstances. He feared lawlessness and social instability. He might today have roundly criticized tactics (of what are called "*andolan jeevis!*" i.e. professional agitators) that resort too quickly to street protest or shutdowns, preferring instead legislative and judicial routes.

Sastri, like some early Indian liberals, operated in a socially elite, English-educated world. Some critics today, we see in fact, often accuse *"Indian liberalism"* of a similar disconnect with broader public sentiment. Sastri too might have found that that some of today's liberal leaders lack deep grassroots ties or rely too much on symbolic posturing.

Sastri championed inclusive *Indian-ness,* moral public leadership, and the dignity of all. But he equally placed real weight on education, self-restraint, and personal example—not just *rhetoric.* He might have gone and supported today's broad calls for protecting *India's "soul"* (understood as *secular, plural, and just*) but would have surely expected rigorous self-discipline and principled action, *not mere slogans.*

Sastri would also today have offered critical fellowship to some modern liberal politicians in India—defending *genuine constitutionalism, civil liberty, women's and minority rights, and pluralist values.* But he would have been sharply critical of those whose *liberalism* lacked depth, principle, or respect for legal methods, and those who used the language of the ***"soul of India"*** as a convenient substitute for real reform or civil behaviour. He would certainly have stood as a formidable reminder that true liberalism is lived practice, not just a platform.

**** ****

Sastri's Views on **Secularism** contrasted with that of Nehru's:

Sastri: Emphasized inclusive secularism based on constitutional equality and mutual respect among religions. He firmly believed in religion but that it should be a private matter, and citizens should act as individuals, not based on exclusive religious identities. Warned against communalism and political divisions based on creed, stressing Hindu-Muslim unity as essential for peace and progress. His secularism was moderate, pluralistic, and sought harmony through understanding.

Nehru: Saw secularism as essential to modern nation-building and governance but was **more explicitly atheist or sceptical of religion's role in public life**. Defined secularism as freedom for all religions to practice so long as they do not interfere with each other or the state's basic functioning. He was personally sceptical about religion's role in public affairs but respected all religions, envisioning a state that keeps a *"principled distance."* Opposed religious communalism and favoured nation-building based on modern, scientific principles. Practiced a pragmatic secularism balancing state neutrality with protection of minority rights.

**** ****

Was the Rt. Hon'ble. Srinivasa Sastri a *Socialist?*

Sastri was fundamentally a **liberal** rather than a **socialist**. His economic views reflected a belief in free enterprise and constitutional progress, but with a strong emphasis on justice, social reform, and gradual political change. While supportive of constitutional reforms and social upliftment, Sastri's vision aligned more with free enterprise and economic liberalism within a framework of fairness rather than socialist or collectivist economic models. Sastri was thus what is defined as a *classical liberal* in economic outlook: supportive of *free enterprise, rule of law, and gradual reform, opposing socialism's more radical redistribution or state control ideas.* His engagement with international diplomacy further reflected a worldview respecting property rights and liberal economic principles, unlike socialist economic planning.

**** ****

If Sastri lived today in India, would he be regarded as a political anachronism?

Sastri's liberal-humanism bears far more resemblance to "*classical liberalism*" or "*liberal constitutionalism*" than to contemporary "***neo-liberalism***" in India or abroad. He stands truly closer to 19th and early 20th century *political* liberals than to late 20th or 21st century *economic* neo-liberals.

Sastri's liberalism was a broad, constitutional, political, and social program. Neo-liberalism is *primarily* an economic program, often with less focus on social equality or political rights. Sastri's genre of liberalism was deeply invested in social uplift, minority rights, and constitutional protection—the *opposite* of the more technocratic, market-dominated outlook of modern neo-liberalism. There's little evidence that Sastri espoused the unfettered free-market economics or anti-state values characteristic of neo-liberalism.

Sastri if he lived today would probably be severely rebuking public figures who, in his view, called themselves liberals but sought power, office, or foreign approval rather than real reform. He would be telling them that he believed showy gestures or slogans (cliches like "*progress*", "*freedom*", "*soul of India*" etc.) were hollow without an ethical core and consistent effort. Sastri would have been sceptical of politicians who paraded liberal ideas for image or electoral gain, rather than embodying those values—and calling instead for policy, humility, and service.

Sastri's values of liberal constitutionalism, pluralism, social justice, and internationalism would very likely place him in opposition or serious critique of the *Hindutva* movement too. He would have been advocating for an India that embraces all its diversities and upholds a constitutional, inclusive democracy.

So yes, Srinivasa Sastry, if he were living amongst us today in India would be looked upon as a *political anachronism.*

While his principles would be held up as being profoundly relevant today and might even earn respect across political lines ... all mere lip-service, no doubt ... the current political environment in India—*with its intensity, fragmentation, dog-eat-dog rivalry and ideological battles*—would quickly and most certainly marginalize a figure of his nuanced, moderate character. Sastri would today remain as much a ***respected outsider*** as he was in his own times. He would never be regarded as a mainstream party leader or influencer.

This overall assessment of Rt. Hon'ble Srinivasa Sastry, the man and the politician should surprise or offend no one ... least of all admirers of Sastri like myself ... because this pattern, of principled moderates being utterly sidelined in favour of our more combative, identity- and electorally-driven breed of politicians, is very common worldwide and it only exemplifies the challenges if not the impossibility of ever upholding true liberal values in contemporary democracies.

**** ****

Sastri's last days in life were spent in his home in the tranquil neighbourhood of Mylapore, Madras. He loved Mylapore. He was happy to breathe his last there... Does Mylapore still remember and cherish his memory today as it did then?

**** **** ****

Chapter 19
The Last Days...

The last days of Srinivasa Sastri were spent in his home "***Swaagatham***" in Mylapore, Madras, one of the oldest, historically the most well-known quarters of the city (now *Chennai*).

Mylapore was indeed one of the oldest and culturally richest neighbourhood in Madras, known for its ancient places of Saivite and Vaishnavite worship, classical music halls, drama auditoriums, "*bhajana-sampradaya*" and above all, notable Tamil and Sanskrit scholarship. Sastri, a scholar deeply versed in Sanskrit, Tamil, and Indian traditions, found in Mylapore a vibrant and spiritually salubrious environment since it nurtured his innate love for *classical learning, religious harmony, and cultural continuity*.... all his core *brahmin-liberal* values in life.

Mylapore was also home to many of his close and dear friends and contemporaries in its intellectual and political elite circles, often called the *"Mylapore Clique,"* who were all known for their scholarly and professional pursuits and contribution to the Indian National Freedom movement. They all had much like Sastri embraced the politics of moderation and constitutional methods.

Alladi Krishnaswami Aiyer *(1883-1953)*

Sastri's own residence and the work he did were both closely linked to this Mylapore cultural milieu, which influenced his sense of identity and intellectual pursuits. The rich temple traditions, festivals, and cultural activities of Mylapore embodied the same *"Sanatana Dharma"* values that Sastri so deeply respected and avidly promoted.

Mylapore was a place where classical Carnatic music, literature, and religious discussions thrived, all which Sastri himself patronised and supported through active engagement with scholars, poets, and institutions. The influence of Mylapore provided a very conducive cultural grounding for Sastri's approach to nationalism and gradualist reform, blending respect for tradition with modern education and civic values. Here is how he said that he felt about his own home in Mylapore:

> *"In the sacred streets of Mylapore, where temples and scholars alike rise in enduring testament to our culture, lies a living testament to India's spiritual and intellectual heritage.* ***This ambience nurtures not only faith but reason;*** *it inspires us to pursue knowledge with humility and serve with diligence." "Let us remember, in these sacred environs where poetry and song ring out, that the work of the mind and the work of the spirit go hand in hand. Mylapore and her scholars gift us this example, and we should cherish it as a beacon for all India."*

In Sastri's time, as it is even today, Mylapore was famed for its religious ambience... the Kapaleeshwara Temple being the most magnificent cynosure of it. Sastri was *a man of both Reason and Faith* at the same time, and he found it easy to soak in and luxuriate himself in that ambience.... It was truly *la dolce vita* of Mylapore! Kodanda Rao, Sastri's biographer's quote below reveals the religious side of the man:

QUOTE:

The doctrine of **Bhakti**, as revealed in the *Gita*, captivated his (Sastri's) heart, but not his head. Sastri said: *"The struggle between the head and the heart, described with self-revelatory pathos in religious writings, rages perpetually within me. It is only my lifelong practice of self-control that cloaks the gnawing of my inmost being behind a blank expression of face."* He craved for some experience, some revelation, some authentic sign of life after death. He had moments when he preferred the contentment of the pig in the sty to the agitation and turmoil of the enquiring mind. But he soon found consolation and encouragement in the thesis that *"there is more faith in honest doubt than in half the creeds"* and concluded that to believe what was not proven to one's satisfaction was to abdicate the sovereign quality of reason.

UNQUOTE

Sastri himself did like to go on occasions to worship in temples since he regarded *"The temple is not merely a place of ritual; it is a centre of art, philosophy, and community. The centuries-old traditions of Mylapore have taught me that our past is not to be preserved as a museum but lived as a fountain of inspiration for modern progress."*

Sastri's house in Mylapore thus became a beehive of cultural activity and a watering-hole for neighbourhood cognoscenti. The home called "*Swaagatham*" became known for being an informal gathering spot for intellectuals, where figures from different disciplines—poetry, politics, philosophy—met for lively, spirited discussions.

"At irregular intervals, a small group of persons interested in public affairs would assemble at Sastri's home in Mylapore. Sastri would listen thoughtfully, speaking only occasionally but with great weight and precision. His calm deliberations often steered conversations towards reason and reconciliation."

**** ****

In his last days in Mylapore, Sastri's engagement with politics and world affairs was reduced to a bare minimum. Even amongst friends who gathered at his house for intellectual conversations with him, he spoke more on literary, art, music and cultural topics than politics. However, there were two specific matters that did catch Sastri's attention and on which he did make known his mind. On one matter his comments went public because it concerned an international issue. The other matter, which was a local issue, he chose to make his comments privately.

The first issue was the advent of the (A) **Apartheid Regime in South Africa** and the second matter was the emerging (B) **Dravidian Movement of the Justice Party of Tamil Nadu** led by **E.V. Ramaswamy Naicker** (aka "*periyaar*").

As mentioned, (already in an earlier chapter) while he had served in South Africa as *Agent-General for the British Government of India*, Sastri had recognized the plight of the Indian community there that was being deprived of even basic human and civil rights. Their plight was an incipient symptom of the growing racial problem in that country. Even as early as 1927–1929, Sastri had already been acutely aware of the dire fate that awaited the Indian community under *White Minority Rule*, and he had consistently advocated for their upliftment as quickly as possible so that they could demand equal treatment as full citizens. He strongly opposed policies treating Indians as aliens or pushing for their repatriation, calling instead for improvements in housing, sanitation, education, and legal status.

Though the formal system of *apartheid* was officially instituted only after Sastri's time in South Africa, his diplomatic efforts and public statements condemned the sort of racial segregation and legal discrimination that was the driving force behind apartheid ideology. He had worked tirelessly to negotiate better rights for Indians and opposed any legislation that legitimized racial inequality.

Now, from Mylapore, he spoke publicly to condemn *Apartheid Rule* in *South Africa* in a manner reminiscent of an impassioned speech on **Legal and Civic Rights**, he had given once in the past:

> *"It is neither justice nor reason to treat the Indian community as aliens in a land that many of us have called home for generations. The laws that seek to exclude us, to restrict us, to repatriate us, are unjust and must be resisted through all means consistent with constitutional dignity.* ***We reject every form of racial segregation, and we demand the recognition of equal rights before the law."***

The speech thus directly condemned the nascent apartheid structure of racial segregation and exclusionary laws, calling for equal legal rights.

(B) Sastri's political career had already peaked in the decades before the **Dravidian Movement** became a dominant force in Tamil Nadu. By the time the *Self-Respect Movement* gathered momentum in the late 1920s and 1930s—and especially when **Dravida Kazhagam (DK)** emerged in the 1940s—Sastri was already an aging figure, focused solely on constitutional advocacy, diplomacy, and liberal reform. He spent some of his later years deeply involved in public education, language debates, and literary activity, rather than frontline political activism in either India or in what became later the State of Tamil Nadu.

The *Dravidian Movement* was openly critical of both the *"Hindu orthodoxy"* and *"nationalist"* positions, seeing both as protecting ***Brahminical*** privilege and ***Sanskritic*** traditions. Periyar's activism aimed thus to counteract what he saw as *"Brahmin superiority"* promoted by Congress moderates, including leaders like ***Sastri*** and **Alladi Krishnaswami Aiyer**.

The main documented response of the *liberal Brahmin* elite (such as Sastri, Krishnaswamy Iyer and Sivasamy Iyer) towards the Dravidian and anti-Brahmin movements was one of **disapproval and quiet reservation**, often articulated in private correspondence or moderate platforms rather than combative public debate. There are secondary and references in the Dravidian Movement literature to "*Brahmin leaders*", including Srinivasa Sastri, upholding social separation and traditional values, which Periyar and the Dravidian ideologues criticized vehemently. Mahatma Gandhi himself recognized the parochial and casteist underpinnings of Periyar's *Self-Respect Movement* and expressed his alarm at the spectre of narrow, sub-national "**identity politics**" beginning to loom large in the State of Madras:

> *"The Justice Party... opposed Brahmins in civil service and politics, and this anti-Brahmin attitude shaped many of its ideas and policies... Gandhi responded by highlighting his appreciation of Brahmin contribution to Hinduism and said, **'I warn the correspondents against separating the Dravidian south from Aryan north. The India today is a blend not only of two, but of many other cultures.'"***

Sastri and his Mylaporean colleagues like Alladi Krishnaswami Aiyer and Sivasami Iyer represented traditional Brahminical values in their public comportment, moral philosophy, and literary emphasis—which stood in implicit, if not explicit, contrast to the Dravidian critique. They came to symbolize—for critics and Dravidian polemicists—an older establishment whose influence was now being actively challenged, not so much in direct confrontation, but through structural social shifts and new populist mobilisations in the streets and public squares.

From his home in Mylapore, which was itself witnessing the winds of change in its traditional and cultural ethos from *liberalism* to increasing *Tamil parochialism,* Sastri might have silently brooded over his foreboding of a grim future for the Tamils of Madras State —- a future where Periyar's "*movement would not work out too well for the Brahmin who would be made the scapegoat for 500 years of Tamil decline slowly unfolding itself...,*" as he once put it.

Sastri sensed that the earliest manifestations of the Dravidian movement was not particularly rabid or secessionist but was more focused on resentment of Brahmin ascendance, particularly in provincial government and education. Yet he feared that the Movement had embedded in it the seeds of secessionism.

Sastri did not however personally engage in any documented direct commentary or confrontation with E.V. Ramaswamy Naicker or the *Dravidian Movement.* His moderate, liberal reformism and devotion to Sanskritic culture stood in intellectual opposition to the radical *anti-Brahmin politics of Periyar,* but their interaction was one of contrast, not direct conflict or debate.

**** ****

In the years and decades to come, the ethos of cultural and intellectual excellence of Sastri's beloved Mylapore would surely undergo a sea-change. It would be able to neither resist nor overcome the ideological onslaught that the Dravidian Movement would come to inflict upon so-called "*Brahminical*" social order and its avowed values of liberalism that Sastri and his "*Mylapore Clique*" had always espoused and wished to propagate.

Inevitably, the time to depart from such a fast-crumbling old-world order was fast approaching... even as Sastri's *angina pectoris* attacks were becoming more frequent and more painful.

**** **** ****

Chapter 20:
"Death of a Brahmin-Liberal"

Indian Express

Rt. Hon'ble Sastri Passes Away

Sudden Peaceful End

AZAD MEETS CABINET MISSION

Congress Position Clarified Further

On **February 19, 1945,** the anniversary of the death of Gopala Krishna Gokhale, Sastri spoke for about forty-five minutes at a public-meeting and suddenly lost consciousness. When he regained it after a while, he was advised by his doctors to give up all arduous work including public speaking.

Nevertheless, on **March 6. 1945,** he gave a press interview about reform of **The Hindu Code**, which was under public discussion then across the country. The question was: did the legislature have the right to deliberate and decide upon issues that were religious in nature and, hence, ought to be left only to the Hindu religious orthodox leaders.

Sastri argued saying in his view the legislature, as then constituted, was competent for the purpose and that some of the suggested reforms were unobjectionable and even necessary. He made his position clear: while the objections raised by the Hindu orthodoxy should he heard with respect and their pleas also must be met as far as possible, the reforms, in their essentials, should not be sacrificed. He was also confident, Sastri said, that Hindu religious orthodoxy had a remarkable capacity to adjust itself to the reforms after enactment, although their capacity to see the need for them during the lead up to the enactment might suggest apparent inflexibility.

Sastri, ever the *Brahmin Liberal-Humanist* that he was, by that singular statement showed that he possessed not only a very acute but also accurate understanding of the Hindu psyche and its religious leaders; that they would baulk at the reformative moves in the beginning but in the end, that they in their wisdom, would come around to accepting and accommodating reforms if found to be reasonable and in the larger good of the country.

in his biography, Kodanda Rao writes, that *"even the mild exertions involved in giving that interview by Sastri, however, took toll on his health. He had a severe heart attack which lasted some three hours. He could not sleep and had to be administered sedatives".*

**** ****

In the biography written by D.V. Gundappa is to be found an endearing anecdote on the end that was fast nearing Srinivasa Sastri.

One day as he lay weak in his sick bed at "*Swaagatham*", his home on V.M. Street, Mylapore, Sastri expressed a desire to listen to Tyagaraja's Kriti "*Paahi Raama-chandra-Raaghava...*" in the Carnatic *Raaga* of *Yadukula Kaambhodhi* rendered by one of Sastri's favourite musicians, **Sri Musiri Subramanya Iyer**. The song was played for him, at his frail bidding, on a 78-rpm gramophone disc. Sastri closed his eyes and was utterly engrossed in listening to the poignant lyrics of the song wherein Saint Thyagaraja beseeches Sri Rama to save him:

> "*O Lord Rama Chandra! O Lord Raghava! O Consort of Sita! O Lotus Eyed! O Lord Rama – worthy of praise by those highly reputed! O Lord worshipped by Emperors! O Ruler of this Thyagarajan!*
>
> *There is none to protect me and nowhere is a God better than You, so please protect me. As You are my refuge, please come, protect me quickly.*
>
> *Is it possible that, no matter how much I entreat You, you would not have even a little mercy towards me? I entreated You to relieve my troubles because I considered You to be the Lord, my most beloved. Please save me quickly because what is the use of life bereft of Your grace?*

Does my appeal seem to You to be a plaything? Otherwise, what could be the nature of my fate? You test me but am I worthy of Your tests? There is no time to delay any further, because I will not go begging for Your Grace at any sundry place (when I have come to you directly)!"

After the song ended on the gramophone-player, Sastri opened his eyes, moist with tears, and whispered softly... "*Can it be played again for me please?... I want to listen to the song once more.....*"

This story has been recorded and is widely cited as a testament to Sastri's devotion to classical music and the personal spiritual resonance of *Bhakti* that he found and cherished so much in Tyagaraja's inspiring compositions.

**** ****

Early in **January 1946**, with his cardiac condition worsening, Sastri was advised to get admitted into the *Madras General Hospital.* Mahatma Gandhi, who was on a visit to Madras, took time off from his hectic public engagements, to call on him in the Hospital on **January 22** and was permitted to be with him for a few minutes.

The meeting was most moving, according to the biographical accounts.

Sastri, who was reclining in bed, sat bolt upright and moved towards the edge of the bed and extended his hands towards the Mahatma and said in a voice choked with emotion:

"I want to come near enough to hug you, little brother!"

In soothing tones, the Mahatma begged Sastri not to excite himself and helped him to recline in bed as Sastri held the Mahatma's hands in both his own.

With great effort, Sastri expressed his disappointment then with Gandhi's no-show at the **Simla Peace Conference** that the British Government had organized in the aftermath of World War-2. The *Conference* was convened by the Viceroy, Lord Wavell, at the Viceregal Lodge in **June-July 1945**. Its primary aim was to facilitate Indian self-government after World War II, as Britain was preparing to leave India. Lord Wavell proposed a new *Executive Council* for India with a majority of Indian members (except the Viceroy and the Commander-in-Chief) and representation for major communities, including Hindus, Muslims, and other minorities. All portfolios except Defence would be controlled by Indians.

Gandhi however had refused to participate in the *Simla Peace Conference* because its Agenda failed to meet the main Congress demands for genuine transfer of power and full independence. The other major sticking point was over the appointment of Muslim representatives—Congress insisted it had the right to nominate Muslims delegates, but the Muslim League was adamant about having the sole right to appoint Muslim representatives. When this deadlock wasn't resolved, Congress viewed the whole process as British-Muslim conspiratorial design to divide Indian unity and was unwilling to participate unless the issues were addressed on their terms. More broadly, Gandhi had grown wary of British offers after failed previous protracted negotiations (like the "*Cripps Mission*", for example), seeing them all as inadequate, piecemeal gestures that wouldn't lead directly to real independence or unity.

So, Sastri lying in a hospital bed virtually awaiting the hour of death, told Gandhi:

"I have wanted to say one thing to you. Another opportunity for peace has been lost. They are sitting there at the Peace Conference Table. But who is there to speak for humanity except you? I am afraid India has failed to do her duty. Even if they do not ask you, you must go as the apostle of truth and non-violence and be on the spot. Your mere presence will have a tremendous effect. You must not stand on ceremony."

Mahatma gently reminded Sastri that he did not come to the hospital to discuss politics with him. Sastri then jokingly retorted: ***"I see, you think I am no longer good enough for it."***

After exchanging further pleasantries, the Mahatma left, knowing that Sastri's end, sadly, was very imminent.

**** ****

The above meeting between Sastri and Mahatma Gandhi is glowing testimony indeed to their lifelong friendship and obvious love for each other as kindred souls. But then in many other less obvious ways the meeting not only forebode Sastri's death but also the death of ***Brahmin Liberalism*** in the Independent India of the future.

In the grindingly long history of the Indian freedom struggle, Sastri had come to be known as an exemplar of the "*vita contemplativa*" as well as the "*vita activa*".

As explained (already in an earlier chapter), for Sastri it had meant a life lived adhering steadfastly to the fundamental tenets of *Sanatana Dharma*... He had famously averred that "*the Hindu civilization rooted in Sanātana Dharma, has constantly been enriched by* ***brahma*** *and safeguarded by* ***kṣāttra***. For Sastri, essentially that meant, again, a "*contemplative way of life*" focused on intellectual and spiritual reflection i.e. the way of true ***"braahmanic*** living", but also combining itself closely with the "*active way of life*" i.e. engagement with the world through moral virtues, social and economic duties, military work, and practical actions ...

For Sastri, the two *"vita-s"* were entirely reflected in 19th-20th century ideas of "*classical liberalism"*. And such blending of "***brahma***" and "***kṣāttra***" in his own life became definitive **Brahmin Liberalism**.

It was truly the *Brahmin-Liberal* in Srinivasa Sastri that made his dying heart melt with *Brahminical Bhakti* feelings as he lay listening to a *Thyagaraja kriti* while, at the very same time, he also vigorously engaged Gandhi in a debate over the political strategy and tactics he had adopted in the very last stages of the great battle for India's freedom nearing its end in the year 1946.

In the democratic-secular, socio-political discourse of India as we know it today, the term *Brahmin-Liberal* is an outright oxymoron.... meaning that you can either be a *Brahmin* or a *Liberal*, but you cannot be ***both*** because the *"vita brahmin"* and *"vita liberal"* are believed to be as mutually exclusive as "*vita contemplativa*" and "*vita activa*" are in Greek philosophy. In the ideological construct of the Dravidian South, especially in Tamil Nadu of which Sastri was a proud native, the Brahmin is today regarded as an *extremist-protagonist* of *Sanatana Dharma* while the Dravidian-Liberal is his *extremist-antagonist.*

Srinivasa Sastri's life though was anything but that of an *extremist* in any sense of the word imaginable... He simply defied the myth which latter-day vicious political propaganda has been purveying -- that a true Brahmin can never be a true Liberal... and that *Dravidian Secula*r culture and *Sanatana Dharma*... "*never the twain shall meet*". Sastri's imminent death thus would signify, sadly, a *fin de siècle* moment for *Brahmin Liberalism* too.

Even upon his deathbed, never would Sastri have given in to maudlin lamentation. We cannot imagine Sastri saying to his friend and compatriot, Mahatma Gandhi: *"Après nous, le déluge, mon ami"* (*"after you and I pass on, dear friend, the deluge shall come...*) ... But it is not unlikely that Sastri, while silently preparing for his end, might found himself brooding: *"Après moi la décadence morale"*....

With the death of "*Classical Liberalis*m", a general moral decadence descended upon a new era in free India?

**** ****

The two biographies – of Gundappa and Kodanda Rao -- continue to narrate to us on how the last days of Sastri unfolded.

The Mahatma, with several friends, called on Sastri again on **January 30, 1946.**

Sastri hailed his friend as the greatest man living and a blessing to him in a hundred ways. The Mahatma protested. Whereupon Sastri quoted a shloka from the "Ramayana" which said that he who did not see Rama or whom Rama did not see was despised by everyone in the world. He (Sastri) spoke of his trance the previous day when he had written a beautiful essay on the episode when Sita persuaded Hanuman to spare from his wrath the minions of Ravana who merely had carried the orders of their master in humiliating her (during her days in captivity in Lanka); they were not guilty themselves.

It was forgiveness, said Sita, which made life worth living. Forgiveness was divine and was the noblest of virtues. None was so free from error that he did not need to be forgiven. She regretted that there were not two or three people who dared to tell the truth to Ravana, the King of Ceylon, and save him from wrongdoing.

Turning to the Mahatma, Sastri said: "That is the duty we owe to friends, and we fail to discharge. I have done that for you once or twice, and as for you,

you do it and sometimes publicly, much to the consternation of everybody. But it is the noblest office of friendship."

**** ****

The Mahatma paid a third visit to Sastri though he had only three hours to spend in Madras and had several engagements to fulfil. It was a Monday, when the Mahatma usually observed *'mouna vrata'* or silence. Therefore, while Sastri talked, the Mahatma replied by writing on paper. Deeply moved, Sastri said:

"Brother, you have done me an exceptional honour, especially by paying this visit when you were in a great hurry. You are nearer and dearer to me than my own brothers, sons and other members of the family. We have come together by some inner affinity. No external reason can explain our friendship. Gokhale was but the occasion of it."

He became breathless with emotion. The Mahatma waved Sastri a fond farewell and went away.

Sastri's health steadily and gradually grew worse. He passed away at 10.35 p.m. on **April 17. 1946.** He was conscious till about fifteen minutes before the end and was speaking to the members of his family. He then lost consciousness and did not regain it.

The news appeared in the morning papers on the **18th** (*The INDIAN EXPRESS*) and a stream of relatives, friends and admirers called at his house "*Swaagatam*" to pay their last respects. His mortal remains were cremated according to orthodox Brahminical rites.

**** ****

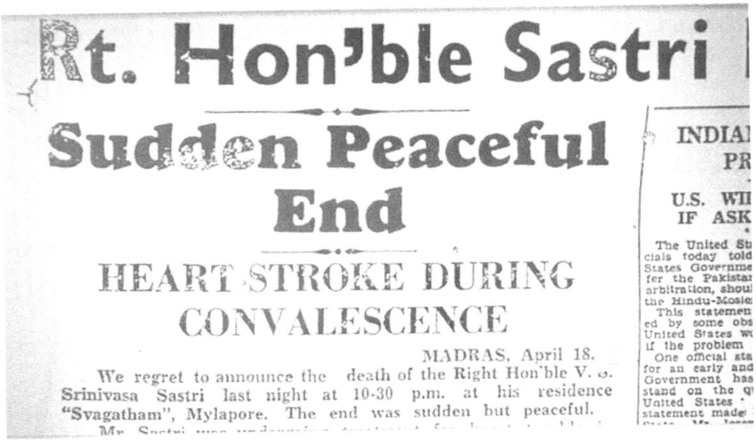

Rt. Hon'ble Sastri

Sudden Peaceful End

HEART STROKE DURING CONVALESCENCE

MADRAS, April 18.

We regret to announce the death of the Right Hon'ble V. S. Srinivasa Sastri last night at 10-30 p.m. at his residence "Svagatham", Mylapore. The end was sudden but peaceful.

The "***"Après moi la décadence morale"*** prediction seemed to come almost true on the very day Srinivasa Sastri passed away... *in a sort of biblical way...*

It was strange, inexplicable why no official mourning or condolence messages were issued by ***British Commonwealth*** leaders when news of Srinivasa Sastri's death became public. Although he was internationally respected through his sterling work as India's *Agent-General in South Africa*, his participation in the *League of Nations*, and diplomatic engagements in Britain and the Dominions, the published obituaries and tributes that were reported in the newspapers following Sastri's death did not focus on Sastri's death as much as they did much later in the year 1948 on Mahatma Gandhi's own. There is no record of formal messages from Commonwealth or any other foreign government heads.

The mourning and tributes after Sastri's death that became public were primarily from leading Indian statesmen, reformers, and public intellectuals, most notably Gandhi and contemporaries in the liberal nationalist tradition. The news-report in *The Indian Express* below is a revealing list of who were true Sastri admirers.

"A century of Indian life has been brought to a close with his passing away," was the tribute paid by Sir S. V. Ramamurthi, Adviser to H. E. the Governor of Madras, when he called at 'Swagatam.'

One of the earliest callers was Sir Lionel Leach, Chief Justice of the Madras High Court. Among the other callers were Mrs Rukmini Arundale, Mr. C. Jinarajadasa, President of the Theosophical Society, Mrs. Baghirathi Sriram, Kumararajah Sir M. A. Muthiah Chettiar of Chettinad, Sir Alladi Krishnaswami Iyer, Sir Vepa Ramesam, the Hon. Mr. Justice B. Somayya, the Hon. Mr. Justice N. Chandrasekhara Iyer, the Hon. Mr. Justice C. N. Kuppuswami Iyer, the Hon. Mr. Justice P. V. Rajamannar, Mr. K. Srinivasan, Mr. Ramnath Goenka, Mr. C. R Srinivasan, Mr. S. Venkateswaran, Mr P. S. Viswanathan, Mr. G. Venkateswaran, Mr. S. Y. Krishnaswami, Mr. K Rajah Iyer, Mr. G. A. Natesan, Mr. T. R Venkatarama Sastri and Lt.-Col. S. P. Sarvadhikhari, Postmaster-General.

The major portion of the last rites were performed at the 'residence itself according to strict Brahminical custom with the assistance of a host of Brahmin priests by Mr. V. S. Sankaran, the only son of Mr. Sastri.

Exactly at 9-30 the funeral procession started, Messrs. G. Sundaram, S. Narayanaswami, T. R. Venkatarama Sastri and Dr. V. Raghavan acting as "pall-bearers."

The reason why neither the British Government nor the British Commonwealth leaders of the world sent in condolence messages on Sastri's death is most likely because they knew that Sastri had always been and still was the *"eternal outsider"* of Indian politics and especially of the *Indian National Congress* with whom momentous negotiations for India's Independence were still underway then and, in fact, were poised at a very critical stage. The British officials knew well that many of the top leaders of the INC – except Gandhi – nurtured no more than barely cordial collegial relations with Sastri. The British Government, thus, at that point in time, did not wish to irritate or in any way embarrass leaders like Nehru, Rajaji or Patel by sending in condolences expressing encomiums for Srinivasa Sastri who, in many ways, had often chosen to oppose their programs, positions and ideas in mainstream politics.

**** ****

What about the three foremost leaders of the INC, then? Did they condole Sastri's passing away?

While none of the three leaders – Nehru, Sardar Vallabhbhai Patel and Rajaji -- is known to have spoken of Sastri with any personal spite, politically he had been often a source of embarrassment for them. They acknowledged that he was an eminent Indian statesman; that certainly he was gifted with rare oratorical skills and that his international stature was legendary. Nevertheless, the three leaders could not quite erase from their collective consciousness the fact that Sastri had taken positions which in the post-Quit India period the Congress Party wanted to leave far behind as just very bad memories.

So, Nehru, Patel and Rajaji chose to maintain public silence over the death of Sastri. No public condolence was expressed by any of them… not a word! It was deliberate, calculated distancing from Sastri's political principles and precepts.

Available public records and major biographical sources today do not show evidence that **Jawaharlal Nehru, C. Rajagopalachari (Rajaji), or Vallabhbhai Patel** made notable public condolence statements specifically reported or widely cited at the time of Sastri's passing. Their individual official condolence messages—if they were published—are not prominent in standard accounts or referenced in major archives.

Similarly, there are no readily accessible records or major press coverage of an official message of condolence issued by the **Indian National Congress** upon Sastri's death. The absence of well-documented, widely reported condolence messages from these leaders of the INC does create a striking and disappointing impression on our minds today. All three leaders had known Sastri personally for decades; Rajaji had even enjoyed an ongoing personal acquaintance with him in Madras. Yet none of them went on public record to condole the death of Sastri. And that lapse on their part can today certainly be read as a lapse in statesmanlike generosity — at least in symbolic and historical sense.

**** ****

Publicly acknowledging the passing of a figure like Sastri would have been both an act of personal respect and a recognition of his contribution to India's public life. It is possible the three leaders may have expressed condolences privately, in closed meetings, or via less-publicised statements that were never picked up by national newspapers and thus never entered the durable historical record. The political climate of early 1946 was certainly extremely intense — negotiations with the British, the Cabinet Mission's arrival, and the approach of independence and partition all dominated the leaders' time and public messaging. Sastri by then was far from the political mainstream, which may have made his passing less of a media priority and for the INC and other national leaders. That said, from a moral perspective, however, the lack of visible tribute does inevitably appear *ungenerous* and hence appears to have been the inauguration of the era of "***la décadence morale***" in India… in a sort of *biblical way…*

In denying the Sastri family as much as a perfunctory message of condolence on their bereavement, the *Indian National Congress* and its three most eminent leaders, Nehru, Patel and Rajaji, appeared to be also denying everything that he had stood for… And that grievous lapse on their part today seems so reminiscent of the old Biblical story wherein Peter, the apostle, denied he ever knew Jesus the Prophet who was being dragged to his death upon the Cross in Jerusalem.

Jesus had predicted at the *Last Supper* that Peter, his disciple, would deny knowing Him *three times* before the *rooster crowed* the next morning. After Jesus' arrest, Peter followed Him at a distance to the high priest's courtyard where the prophet was going to be arraigned. There amongst the gathering of common onlookers and confronted by a poor servant girl and two others poor peasants who immediately recognized Peter as Jesus's follower, he cowered and denied ever being a disciple of Jesus! *Three separate times* did Peter deny Jesus out of fear that he too might be apprehended by the authorities of the State and dragged to death. After the *third denial*, a *rooster* in the village square was heard *crowing*! And Peter at once remembered Jesus' prophecy. Filled with remorse, Peter went out and wept bitterly.

In Sastri's case, there were *three denials* of similar biblical kind --- one each by Nehru, Patel and Rajaji, who denied Sastri, lain on the funeral pyre, even the courtesy of a message in condolence.

Many of the obituaries for deceased leaders of the great stature of Srinivasa Sastri, especially if received from leaders like Nehru and Rajaji, tended to be reprinted decades later in collected works, biographies, or in the *Collected Works of Gandhi/Nehru/Rajaji*. The fact that no well-documented evidence of such condolences exists in these sources — while Gandhi's note alone is well preserved — strongly suggests one of two possibilities: The lapse had either slipped through somehow historical records. Or these Congress leaders simply did not issue public messages at all — perhaps out of political calculation or deliberation, given Sastri's known opposition to ***Quit India*** and his wartime cooperation with the British. If anything was however said by them at all, it was done in a very minor, perfunctory way, maybe in a local setting, without press release or AICC-INC resolution, so it never entered the durable public record. It simply *"slipped through"*.

Given the norms of the time and the way obituaries for major figures were covered, the second scenario — i.e. *deliberate public silence or near-silence* — seems more plausible than the *"slipped through history"* argument.

What makes the absence of condolences from Nehru, Patel and Rajaji rather morally reprehensible is probably that it reflects a conscious choice rather than an archival accident. It fits with the broader reality that by 1946 Sastri was very much outside the Congress mainstream, and the top leadership was focused on partition negotiations and the Cabinet Mission, not on paying tribute to a man whose politics they regarded as outdated or even unhelpful.

By 1946, for Jawaharlal Nehru, Rajaji, and Vallabhbhai Patel, the Rt. Hon'ble V. S. Srinivasa Sastri represented a political tradition they had not only outgrown but, in some respects, wished to keep away more than merely at arm's length.

**** ****

On the death of Srinivasa Sastri in April 1946, Mahatma Gandhi, however, publicly conveyed his condolence with a heartfelt tribute in the pages of *Harijan*, stating for historical record a stirring one-liner:

"Death has removed not only from us but from the world one of India's best sons."

********* THE END *********

Other books by M.K. Sudarshan published by Blue Rose Publishing

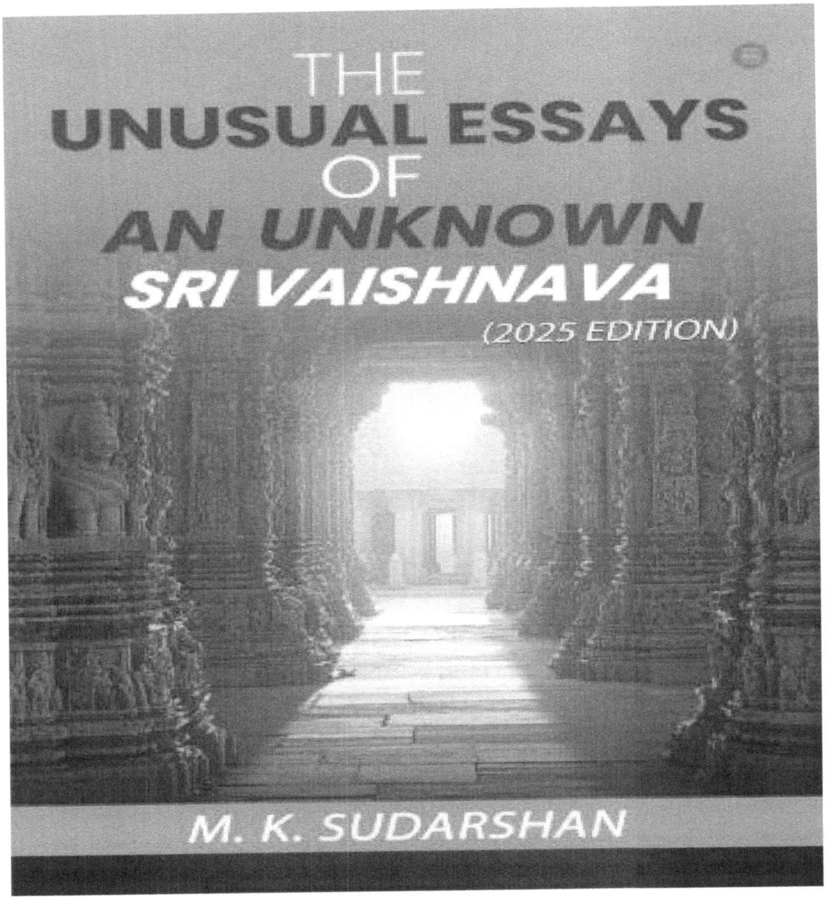

REVIEWS of "The Unusual Essays of an Unknown Sri Vaishnava"
(First Edition: 2016)

"A book of personal essays on subjects related to a particular Hindu sect . . . Many touch on thinkers from the Western canon, as well. William Blake, William Shakespeare, and William Wordsworth all receive mentions, and it's in this blending of influences that the book achieves its unique, inviting perspective . . . Enlightening dive into Sri Vaishnavism."

- KIRKUS INDIE REVIEW (April 2018)
https://www.kirkusreviews.com/book-reviews/mk-sudarshan/unusual-essays-unknown-sri-vaishnava/

" this book is certainly an engrossing read with the most complex of philosophies, practices, culture and other aspects of a global citizen's daily life explained in an engaging yet easily comprehensible style of the author."

Dr M. Varadarajan
"THE HINDU" (August 2017)
(India's National Newspaper since 1878)
http://www.thehindu.com/books/books-reviews/ rituals-associated-with-vaishnavism/article19464016.ece

"The book . . . Has the unique distinction of receiving the blessings and appreciation of the presiding pontiffs of all 3 principal and extant Vedantic schools in India—VisishtAdaita, Advaita and Dvaita: Sri Ahobila Mutt, Sri Sankaraacharya Mutt, Sringeri and Udupi Sri Pejaawar Mutt"

"MYLAPORE TALK", Chennai, Dec 2017

The author brings to bear a refreshingly new focus on various traditional concepts and scriptures while taking care to toe the traditional (Sri Vaishnava) line mostly, . . . With an impeccable language and excellent narrative style . . . this book impresses one with its nice turn of phrases, the facile rendering of even difficult ideas in comprehensible terms . . . This book would form a welcome addition to anyone's library . . . especially useful to expatriate youth of today—it would help them find their traditional spiritual moorings despite being cast adrift in the ocean of international commerce with no polestar to guide them".

—Sadagopan Iyengar, Editor, "Nrsimha Priya":
(Official English Journal of Sri Ahobila Mutt, India - Nov 2016)

INR 1000

BlueRoseONE
Stories Matter
New Delhi • London

RELIGION & SPIRITUALITY

9 789370 181953
www.BlueRoseOne.com

"The Nondescript God: Abstraction or Paragon?"

"The author of this book … has adopted a unique approach to explain the Visishtadvaita perspective of realisation Brahman, in the form of a dialogue between a student and an unknown Sri Vaishnava…. The book is a welcome addition to the learners and scholars of both Advaita and Visishtadvaita philosophies.

M. Varadarajan reviewing in THE HINDU dt. June 17, 2022

"This book explains the uniqueness of the Visishtadvaita interpretation of Theism in contradistinction to the Advaitin's. It's an impressively intense read delving deep into these two streams of Hindu philosophy, but in a nutshell…. (This book) is a jackpot for a theology student or anyone in generally … interested in understanding the dichotomy between Advaita and Visishtadvaita … (It's) a ten on ten!"

The Indian Express dt. August 12, 2022

"…. A welcome addition to Visishtadvaita literature … the book is aimed at those who thirst for 'sampradaayic' knowledge but are handicapped by their lack of acquaintance with Sanskrit or Manipravalam (language) in which most of the scholarly treatises (in Srivaishnavism) have been written."

"Sri Nrisimha Priya": May 2022 issue

"The Nondescript God" is a remarkable book with descriptive analysis and intellectual clarity. I read it twice. It reminded me of Socrates's dialogue! It educates people like me who are caught between modernity and tradition while you (the author) are well-equipped in both."

Indira Parthasarathy (R. Parthasarathy, or Ee. Paa., is an Indian author and playwright who writes in Tamil. He has published 16 novels, 10 plays, anthologies of short stories, and essays; the only Tamil writer to receive both the Sahitya Akademi Award (1977) and the Sangeet Natak Akademi Award (2004). He received Padma Shri in the year 2010, given by Government of India).

"The Epistles of a Prolific Pontiff"

"The Tamil "Arul mozhis" of Srimad Mukkur Azhagiyasingar conveyed lofty matters of Vedanta in easy-to-understand language for the layman. Now, in this book of English translations of the original by Sudarshan, the "Arul mozhis" have been made even more accessible and comprehensible to our younger English-speaking generations who are not so well versed either in Sanskrit or Tamil language…. I pray to Lord Malolan that this book should reach the homes of all those who have faith in the tenets of our Sanatana Dharma."

HH Srimathe Srivan Satagopa Sri Ranganatha Yatindra Mahadesikan (present 46th Pontiff of the Sri Ahobila Mutt)

"Sudarshan has translated into English the Tamil "Arul mozhis" of the great Acharya Srimad Mukkur Azhagiyasingar for the benefit

of those of our younger generations have relocated abroad or away from their native roots. The essays of the Acharya have been translated not just in English language... I would say rather they have been translated by him into sheer poetry..."

Dr. S. Padmanabhacharya, Sri Karyam of Sri Ahobila Mutt and former Head of the Department of Sanskrit and Vaishnavism Studies, Madras University, Chennai, India.

"(Sudarshan) is able to capture the spirit of each Arulmozhi and tell the story in his own words, words which display a nice turn of phrase and make for a smooth, seamless narrative.... It is evident that this has been a labour of love for Sri Sudarshan ... to bring the wonderful words of this spiritual giant to the English-speaking readers without detracting a bit from the tone, tenor and spirit of the original."

- ***K. Sadagopa Iyengar, Editor, Nrisimha Priya***

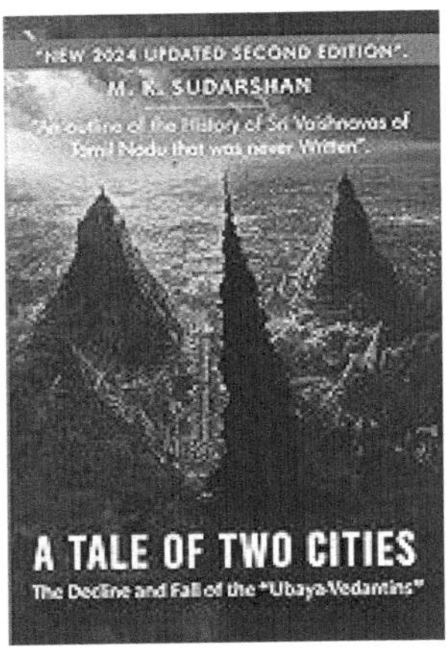

A Tale of Two Cities: The Decline and Fall of the "Ubaya Vedantins" – An Outline of the History of the Sri Vaishnavas of Tamil Nadu that was never written" (2024)

"... the whole the book is a must read for every Hindu whether he or she is a Sri Vaishnava or not. Because this is part of our history and the author has with genuine love for all Hindus, has made this the story with valuable lessons for our future as well."

----- Aravindan Neelakandan

****

"The Middlemen of Vedapura" (fiction): *an English translation of Tamil satirical novel by* ***Indira Parthasarathy*** *(Sahitya and Sangitha Nataka Akademy and Padma Shree Award winning author and playwright)*

"*... the narrative style and portrayal are engrossing. Notwithstanding certain striking similarities to political personalities that the country has seen, The Middlemen of Vedapura should not be viewed as a work that fictionalises real-life incidents. It goes beyond, and the translator has captured the spirit of the work very well.*"

- ***"The Hindu"*** May 23, 2025